Implementing Tableau Server

A guide to implementing Tableau Server

Version 10.x

Chandraish Sinha

www.OhioComputerAcademy.com

Legal Notes

About The Author

Chandraish Sinha has 19 years of experience in implementing Business Intelligence solutions. His experience involves working in different BI applications. He has worked in multiple Tableau end-to-end implementations.

He coaches organizations and consultants in exploring the visualization world of Tableau.

He has a passion for Tableau and shares his knowledge through his blog (http://www.learntableaupublic.com/).

Other books by the author:

1. Tableau 10 for Beginners
2. Tableau Dashboards: Step by Step guide to developing visualizations in Tableau 9.2
3. Tableau Questions & Answers: Guide to Tableau concepts and FAQs
4. QlikView Essentials
5. QlikView Questions and Answers: Guide to QlikView and FAQs
6. How to be a Successful IT Professional in the USA: A Checklist and Easy Guide to Success

Word from the Author

Thank you for providing great support to my books.

My objective, with this book is to explain all the concepts in a simple, easy-to-understand manner.

Your comments help me in improving myself. As always, please do write to me at chandraish@gmail.com. I personally read and respond to all my messages.

Reader feedback

If you enjoyed this book, found it useful, or otherwise, I'd really appreciate if you would post a short review on Amazon. I do read all the reviews personally so that I can continue to improve.

Thanks for your support!

Table of Contents

Preface

An efficiently performing Server is a key for success in any visualization application.
A good understanding of Tableau Server and its functionality will help in providing robust solution to business users.
The Objective of this book is to provide a complete understanding of Tableau Server concepts.
This book explains concepts in a very easy-to-understand manner. It provides direction and guidance for advanced exploration.

About this book

Chapter1. **Overview**
This Chapter provides an overview of Tableau environment, Tableau desktop and Tableau Server.
Chapter2. **Installing Tableau Server**
This chapter will help you in installing the Tableau Server on a single machine and in a distributed environment.
Chapter3. **Tableau Server Workspace**
In this chapter learn all the aspects of Tableau Server User interface.
Chapter4. **Security**
This chapter deals with securing the Tableau server environment.
Chapter5. **Managing Sites**
This chapter provides details on how to create and maintain a Site in Tableau.
Chapter6. **Branding**
This chapter provides information on how to change the look and feel of the Tableau Server interface.
Chapter7. **Performance and Monitoring**
This chapter provides tips on how to improve performance and monitoring of the server.
Chapter8. **Backup and Restore**

This chapter provides details on taking server backup and restoring the server in case of system failure.

Chapter9. **Log files**

This chapter provides details on all the types of log files in Tableau.

Chapter10. **Command Line Utilities**

This chapter provides details on how to use command line utilities viz. tabcmd and tabadmin to manage the server.

Chapter11. **Javascript API**

This chapter provides details on how to use javascript API.

Chapter12. **Managing Content**

This chapter provides details on how to create users, Projects, and Groups. It also details on publishing and securing views. This chapter also provide an overview of web authoring in Tableau.

How to use this Book

This book gives all the concepts related to Tableau Server. To recreate scenarios presented in this book, use **Tableau Server or Tableau Online**.

A two-week trial version of Tableau Server can be downloaded from http://www.tableau.com/products/

The book also makes use of Tableau desktop. Tableau desktop is used to publish data sources and views on the server. Download Tableau desktop from http://www.tableau.com/products/

To gain detailed understanding of designing visualization using Tableau desktop, visit http://www.tableau.com/learn/training for free online videos provided by Tableau. You can also refer my book **Tableau 10 for Beginners**, available on Amazon.

Who needs this book?

This book is for professionals who want to learn about implementing Tableau Server in a business environment. It is useful for Tableau Server administrators, Site Administrators, Developers and Analysts.

Other Resources

http://www.tableau.com/ is a good resource for information on Tableau. Visit http://www.tableau.com/learn/training for free online videos provided by Tableau.

Also visit Author's blog http://www.learntableaupublic.com/ to extend your learning with advanced Tableau concepts and discussions.

1
Overview

Before learning about Tableau Server, let's learn about Tableau software application.

Tableau is a data visualization application created by Tableau Software. Tableau can connect and extract data from various data sources and present them in easy-to-understand charts and tables.

Tableau is a Business Intelligence (BI) application because it can extract raw data, transform it and present in a way that is helpful in making useful decisions.

Tableau comes with a suite of products that cater to different functionalities.

- **Tableau desktop**

  Tableau desktop is used for developing visualizations in the form of Sheets, Dashboards and Stories.

  Other useful functionalities of Tableau desktop are; data transformation, creating data sources, creating extracts and publishing visualization on the Tableau Server. Tableau desktop produces files with extensions twb and twbx.

  It is a licensed product but comes with 2 weeks of trial.

- **Tableau Public**

  It is a free application provided by Tableau to develop visualizations. In functionality, it is similar to Tableau desktop but files are published on https://public.tableau.com and are accessible to everyone.

- **Tableau Server**

  Tableau Server is a central repository for Users, Data sources and Visualizations. Users can interact with the dashboards on the server without any installation on their machines. Tableau server also provides robust security to the dashboards. Tableau Server web-edit feature allows authorized users to download and edit the dashboards. Data refresh jobs can also be scheduled on Tableau Server.

- **Tableau Online**
  Tableau Online is Tableau Server hosted by Tableau on a cloud platform. Tableau Online is a fully hosted solution, organizations don't have to spend resources on configuring hardware, scalability or maintenance.
- **Tableau Reader**
  Tableau Reader is a free desktop application to view and interact with Tableau visualizations. Users can view dashboards saved as twbx.

Tableau Online vs Tableau Server

Tableau Online and Tableau Server provide similar functionalities. If you have to decide between the two, consider the following

Tableau Online

- Tableau Online is a hosted solution provided by Tableau. You purchase subscription based licenses to access dashboards in Tableau Online.
- Hardware and software are outside your firewall.
- If you need additional sites, you have to purchase them separately.
- Tableau Online supports live data connections to only Amazon Redshift, Google BigQuery and SQL based o
- Active Directory authentication is not available.
- h access is not available.

Tableau Server

- Organizations maintain their own hardware and applications inside their firewall.

- Creating additional sites is free.
- You can have live as well as published extracts.
- Security can be implemented using Active directory or any other security mechanism.
- Guess access is allowed.

Overview of Tableau Desktop

Basic understanding of Tableau desktop is essential for Server implementation. This section will provide a brief overview of Tableau desktop. To learn more about Tableau desktop, visit www.Tableau.com or refer my earlier book **Tableau 10 for Beginners**. Link to the book is http://amzn.to/2rXeEPB

Tableau desktop is used to create visualizations in Tableau. Files created in Tableau desktop are called Workbooks (twb or twbx).

To create a visualization in Tableau, install Tableau desktop or Tableau Public from https://www.tableau.com/products. Once Tableau desktop is installed, it will create a folder **My Tableau Repository** under \Documents\My Tableau Repository.

Create an application in Tableau desktop

Create a simple application to understand how Tableau desktop works. This exercise will use Tableau's sample data source, Sample – Superstore.xls.

1. Launch Tableau desktop. It will open up **Connect** window. Here you can connect to any of the available data sources.

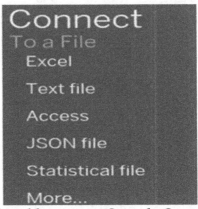

2. Click on **Excel** and browse to Sample-Superstore.xls. This xls will be present in \\Documents\My Tableau Repository\Datasources on your machine.
3. **Connections** windows will be displayed. It displays 3 sheets, because the Sample-Superstore.xls contains 3 sheets. These sheets act as tables. You can use any one or join them as needed.

4. Click on **Orders** and place it into "Drags sheets here"

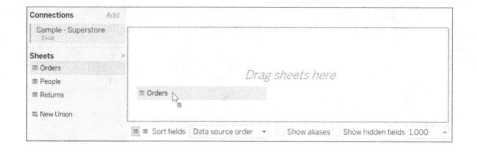

❖ Data Source can be connected as Live or Extract.

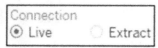

Selecting Extract will create a Tableau Data Extract (TDE) file.

5. Click on Go to Worksheet or Sheet 1 at the bottom of the screen to navigate to the development workspace.

6. Tableau desktop workspace is displayed. On the left pane, Data source **Orders (Sample - Superstore)** is displayed. Data is automatically segregated in dimensions and measures.

7. From the dimensions, double click on **Category** and from the Measures double click on **Sales**. Drop Category on the Color. You will get a visualization like the on below.

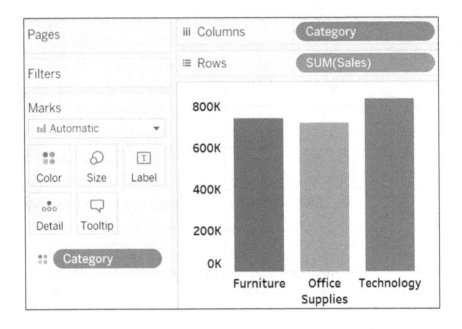

Publishing a data source

In Tableau, data sources and visualizations can be published to the server.

To publish a data source, right click on the Data Source **Orders (Sample - Superstore)** and select **Publish to Server.** It will prompt you for Server login. Server must be installed and configured to publish data source.

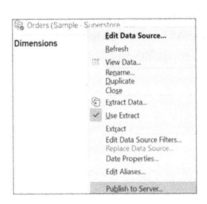

Publishing a Workbook

Tableau desktop is used to publish visualizations can to the Server. You can publish either a twb or a twbx file. Navigate to the main menu/Server and select Publish Workbook. It will prompt you for Server login. Server must be installed and configured to publish a workbook.

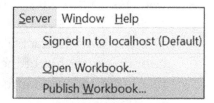

You can publish the entire workbook or specific sheets and dashboards in the workbook.

While publishing a workbook, you have to select a Project. Project is a collection of related workbooks.

You can also assign permissions to the workbooks.

Once workbook is published on the server, authorized users can login to Server URL and access the workbook.

These concepts are discussed in detail in the subsequent chapters.

Important keywords/terms

Keyword/Terms	Description
Twb	Tableau desktop is used to create Tableau workbook (twb) file. It contains data connection and views.
Twbx	Twbx is also a workbook but it is packaged with data. A design file in tableau can be saved as twb or twbx.
TDE	Tableau Data Extract. This data file contains snapshot of the data.
Data source	Connect to a data source to create workbooks.
Tableau Server	Repository of Tableau content i.e. To access tableau server, you will use a URL.
User	User/s are added to the Tableau Server, manually, via csv file or active directory.
Project	Projects are present under Content tab on the Tableau Server. Projects are a collection of related workbooks.
Groups	Users are organized in Groups, in the Tableau Server. A user can belong to one or many Groups.
Site	Site is a logical space in Tableau server. Function of a Site is user and data isolation.
Server Administrator	This user manages all the server resources, grants privileges to Site Administrator
Site Administrator	This user manages specific sites based on the privileges granted by the Server Administrator
Tabcmd	A command line utility program used to automate certain Tableau tasks
Tabdmin	A command line utility program used to execute certain administrative tasks.

Architecture of Tableau Server

Tableau Architecture follows as below

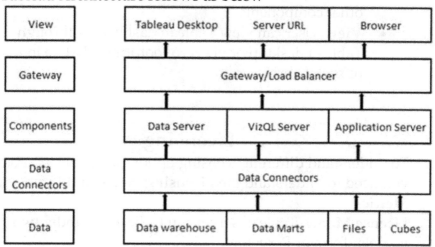

- **Data.** Tableau can connect to any format of source data.
- **Data Connectors.** Tableau provides over 40 optimized data connectors. It can connect to various data sources such as MS Excel, MS SQL Server, Google Big Query, Amazon RedShift, Oracle and others.
- It also provides a generic ODBC connector for systems without a native connector.
  Data can be used in-memory or live.
- **Components.** The following components handle the server operations
    - **Application server.** Application Server processes (wgserver.exe) handle content browsing, Server-Administration and authentication to Tableau server web and mobile interfaces.
    - **VizQL Server.** When a user/client requests a visualization, it sends a request to VizQL process (Vizqlserver.exe). The VizQL process in turn sends queries to the data source, returning a result set in the form of images.

- o **Data Server.** It facilitates the management of Data sources on the server.
- **Gateway/Load balancer.** Gateway directs requests to other components.
- **View.** User can view Tableau dashboards through Tableau desktop or via zero footprint HTML 5 in a web or mobile browser.

Licensing

To understand different licensing options available in Tableau, you need to understand the **Licensing model** and **Licensing Metric**.

License Model. Tableau server can be licensed under two models, Term or Perpetual.

Term Licenses are also called subscription licenses and permit the use of Tableau Server for a period of time.

Perpetual license provide use for unlimited period of time but purchase of support and maintenance is required for continuous access.

License Metric. In addition to License model, Tableau Server license is also governed by License Metric of User-based or Core-based.

User-based or interactor license specify the named users having access to Tableau Server. This works with Tableau Server single machine or cluster installation. The total number of named users should not exceed the license limits.

Core- Based

Core-based license allows Tableau Server to run on a specific number of CPU cores. Tableau Server can be installed on a single machine or a cluster. The number of CPU cores must not exceed the number of cores permitted in the license.

There is no limitation on the number of users utilizing Tableau Server. Even though there is no limitation on the number of users, a set number of cores can support only certain number of users. Number of users per core depends on the usage of the visualization, interaction and data.

Tableau Server Deployment Options

Tableau Server can be installed on a Single-machine or in a multiple-node environment. The type of installation and licensing will depend on the usage and number of users. Tableau Server also allows multi-tenancy i.e. it allows creation of multiple **Sites** on the Server, pertaining to different user groups and content.

Each site has its own URL and its own set of users. Each site has completely segregated users and content. An Organization can have multiple sites, each catering to specific user group and content.

Server Administrators will create Sites and Site Admins will be responsible for administering the Sites.

When Tableau Server is installed, it automatically creates a Site **Default**. On a single-site mode, you use Site "default" without explicitly specifying it but if create multiple sites are created, Default shows up in the list of available Sites.

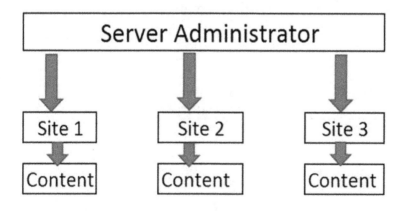

2
Installing Tableau Server

Tableau server is a window based application and requires the following minimum requirements for installation

Supported Operating System	Available in 64-bit versions.	
	Install on Windows Server 2008 or higher	
	Can install on Virtual or physical platforms	
Minimum Hardware Requirements	Server Version 64 –bit	**CPU** 2-8-Core **RAM** 32 GB **Free disk space** 15/50 GB
Administrative Account	The account under which Tableau server must have the permission to install and manage services	
Run as Account	Useful if you are using NT authentication with data sources	

IIS and Port 80	Internet Information Services and Gateway uses Port 80	
Static IP Address	Computer running Tableau Server should have static IP Address	

❖ Production environment of Tableau Server should exceed the minimum requirements.

Tableau Server installation and Configuration will require the following information

- A user account that the service can use. Windows Network Account is used by default. When specifying a user account, domain name, user name and password are required.
- Active directory domain name, if the users will be authenticated via Active directory.
- Option to open the port in windows firewall so that the other machines in the network can access the server.
- Tableau server will require multiple TCP/IP Ports to be available.
- Database drivers, if needed, can be downloaded from http://www.tableau.com/support/drivers

For installing Tableau Server, download the file from http://www.tableau.com/products/server/download

❖ When Tableau Server is installed the first time, you perform initial configuration of the Server as part of the installation. Once initial installation is completed, you can perform additional configuration changes from Tableau

❖ Configuration Utility. This utility will be installed and available on your Start Menu.

Steps

1. Double-click the installation file.
2. Follow the instructions.

    ❖ For local machine install, select the defaults.
    ❖ User authentication setting is one-time setting. select local authentication, if you are not using Active directory.

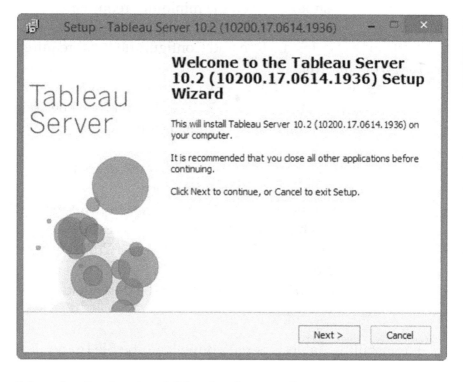

Select the destination folder for the installation. You can leave this as default.

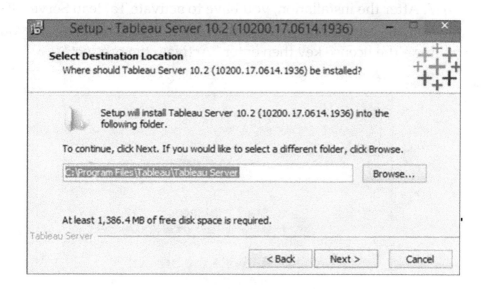

3. System verification will be performed. This will make sure that your machine fulfills the minimum requirement for the installation.

4. Read and accept the License agreement.

5. Short cuts will be created in your start menu.

6. Click Install to Install the application.

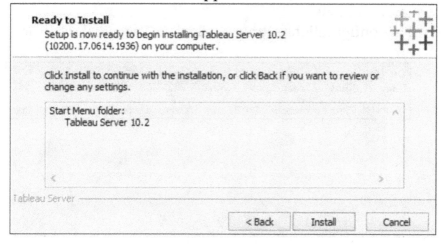

7. After the installation, you have to activate Tableau Server. If you are using a trial version then select "Start trial now". If you have the license key then enter "Activate the product"

8. Tableau Server Configuration options will appear after the activation of the application.
In the initial installation, you will see fewer options; once the installation is completed, you can go to the Tableau Configuration on your machine and make additional configurations.
The configurations setting available in the initial setup are,

⚙	Tableau Server Configuration				
General	Data Connections	SMTP Setup	Alerts and Subscriptions	SAML	OpenID

The following table provides a description on various configuration settings on the Tableau Server configuration

Configuration Tab	Setting	Description
General	User	Windows user name, under which the server will run.
	User Authentication	Active Directory or Local Authentication. This is a one-time entry, cannot be changed later. Use local Authentication, if you are installing on your local machine
	Port number	Default port number is 80
	Open port in windows firewall	Check this box. If the port is not open, the users on another machine will not be able to access the server.
	Server crash reporter	This setting enables the Tableau Server to allow logs and related files to be sent to Tableau when server issues result in crash.
Data Connections	Caching	*Refresh less often* - This option reduces the number of queries sent to the

		database.
		Balanced - Data is removed from the cache after a specified number of minutes
		Refresh more often - The database is queried each time the page is loaded. Not efficient for performance.
	Initial SQL	In workbooks that connect to Teradata, developers can specify commands that will run when the workbook is loaded in the browser. Disable this setting for improved performance.
SMTP Setup		SMTP setup is required for Tableau server to send email alerts to Admins in case of failure.
	SMTP Server	SMTP Server name
	Username/password	Specify username and password, in case SMTP server requires.
	Port	Default port number is 25. Change the port number, if you

		are using a different port.
	Enable TLS	Uncheck this setting to make the connection unencrypted.
	Send email from	Email id that will send alert emails.
	Send email to	Email id that will receive alerts. Multiple emails ids separated by commas can be entered.
	Tableau Server URL	Tableau Server url.
Alerts and Subscriptions	Alerts and Subscription	Check the boxes for the conditions when you want email alerts to be sent.
SAML		SAML settings are used for single sign-on.
OpenID		Configure Tableau Server to support OpenID connect to single sign-in.

Adding an Administrator Account

Once initial installation and configuration are done, an option to create a server administrator account will pop up.
The Administrator will have access to all the Server content and resources.

Adding an Administrator account will differ, depending on whether you have selected Active directory or Local Authentication, while performing the initial setup.
If you are using **Active directory authentication**, type the username and password of the Active directory user who is designated to be the Server Administrator.

If you are using **local authentication**, create an Administrator account by typing Username and password. You can provide any user name and password of your choice.

This book uses the following,
Username   : Administrator
Display name : Administrator
Password   : Admin123

Tableau configuration utility

After the initial installation is completed, you can use Tableau Configuration utility to perform additional changes. Some of the options are available only when you run the Tableau utility after the initial installation.

To run the utility, type **Configure Tableau Server** on your Window's Start menu. To save any changes to the configuration you should Stop the Server. **Stop Tableau Server** can also be located in your windows Start Program.

The following tabs will appear when you run the Tableau Configuration utility. Notice that some additional tabs have appeared this time.

Tableau Server Configuration
General Data Connections Servers SMTP Setup Alerts and Subscriptions SSL   SAML Kerberos SAP HANA OpenID

Configure Servers

Configuration Tab	Setting	Description
Servers	Edit	Use **Edit** to modify the number of process processes for Vizql, Application and so on. Number of processes should be changed to improve performance.
	Add	Use **Add** to add workers to the Tableau Server installation. This is done in distributed

		installation environment, where processes can be run on a different machine.
	Discover	**Discover** is used when you are adding more nodes in a distributed installation.
	Select host	Select the primary host in a distributed installation.
SSL		Tableau Server can be configured to use Secure Sockets Layer (SSL) encrypted communications on all external HTTP traffic. If you are not using this option, check "Off for all connections"
Kerberos		Configuration of Kerberos provide single sign-on experience across all the applications in your organization.If you are not using Kerberos, leave these settings as default or uncheck.
SAP Hana		This configuration allows you to provide a single

		sign-on experience for users making SAP HANA connections.

Once Tableau Server is installed look for the various folders under C:\Program Files\Tableau\Tableau Server\10.2. If you have selected a different installation directory, look under that directory path.

Tableau Server Distributed Installation

In the previous section, Tableau Server single machine installation was performed. Tableau Server can also be installed on multiple machines.

Multi-machine or distributed/Cluster installation helps in managing the load and fail-over of the Server.

Distributed installation involves installing Tableau Server on a primary computer and Tableau Server worker on different machines.

Planning for distributed Installation

- Tableau Server is available in 32-bit and 64-bit versions. Especially the versions prior to Tableau Server 10 come in 32-bit too. When performing distributed installation, primary machine and worker nodes should have the same bit version.
- Identify the computers you plan to have in the cluster. Each computer in the cluster should have a static IP.
- All computers in the cluster should be in the same domain.
- The computers in the cluster should be able to communicate with one other. Refer to the list of default ports used by Tableau server. *The list is provided at the end of this chapter.*
- Each computer should have local admin permissions.
- Download Tableau Server and Tableau Server Worker software from your customer account at https://www.tableau.com/. The trial version does not allow distributed installation.
- For distributed installation Tableau Server – multi-machine core license or user-based license is required.

- For failover support for the data engine and repository processes, at least three computers are required. One for the primary Tableau Server and two for Tableau worker nodes.
- For failover and multiple gateway support, you need four computers. Three computers for failover and one for load balancer.
- For high availability, you will need four computers as described earlier and an additional computer to act as a backup primary for the primary Tableau Server.

Configuring distributed installation

Before performing distributed installation changes, initial installation and setup should be completed on the primary computer.

Steps
1. Install Tableau Server and perform initial setup on the primary machine. Note the IPv4 address or computer name of the primary machine.
2. Stop Tableau Server. To Stop Tableau Server, use "Stop Tableau Server" from start menu.
3. Download Tableau Server Worker software and run Tableau Server Worker Setup on other computers/Workers in the cluster.
4. During installation, provide the primary machine's IPv4 or computer name.
5. Once the worker Software is installed on the worker machines, launch Tableau configuration utility on the Primary machine. To launch Tableau Configuration

6. utility, type "configure Tableau Server" on the primary machine's Start program menu.
7. On Tableau configuration, navigate to the **Servers** tab. Click on **Add** to specify the IPv4 address or computer name of one of the worker machines. Specify the number of services to be run on this worker machine.
   With the 64-bit version of Tableau Worker Server, up to two instances of each service process can be run.

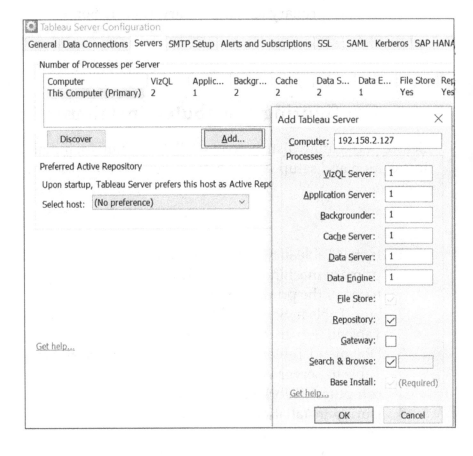

8. Repeat the above steps to add other worker nodes as needed.
9. Click OK to save the settings and start the server.

❖ The installation of Tableau Server and Tableau Server Workers automatically install drivers for Oracle and Oracle Essbase databases. If you plan to connect to other databases, you need to install the corresponding drivers on your primary and worker servers. Workers running VizQL, application server, data server, or backgrounder processes need these database drivers.

A word about Tableau Server Repository

The information about Tableau Server viz. Projects, Groups, Users, Data sources, Workbooks, Views, Extract metadata and refresh information is stored in Tableau Server Repository. It is a PostgreSQL database that stores all of the Server data.
You can connect to Tableau Server repository and create views in Tableau desktop.

You specify the Tableau Server Repository in Tableau Configuration.

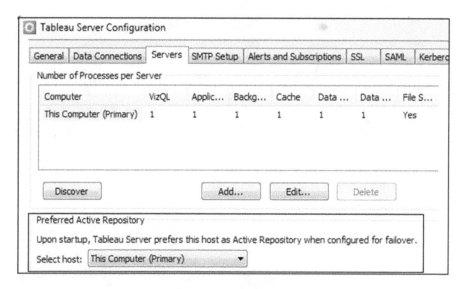

Updating Tableau Server IP

If Tableau Server gets a new IP, you need to update Tableau Server Configuration with the new IP.

This can be done by running tabadmin config command.

Steps

1. On the primary server, launch command prompt as Administrator and type the following command

```
cd "C:\Program Files\Tableau\Tableau Server\10.2\bin"
```

2. Stop the Tableau Server, by using

```
tabadmin stop
```

3. To update Tableau Server configuration , type

```
tabadmin config
```

4. Start the server by typing

```
tabadmin start
```

Uninstalling Tableau Server

Follow the steps below to uninstall Tableau Server
Steps
1. Take a backup of your existing Tableau Server installation. To take the backup, use tabcmd backup command. See chapter Backup and Restore for more details.
2. For a **Single-machine install**, use Add/Remove programs on your Tableau Server machine to uninstall Tableau Server. Uninstalling removes the Tableau Server software, but leaves the data, configuration settings and folder structure on the machine.
3. Manually delete the Tableau Server versioned directory. This directory is located under

C:\Program Files\Tableau\Tableau Server

For a distributed installation, follow the following steps
Steps
1. Take a backup of your existing Tableau Server installation. To take the backup, use tabcmd backup command. See chapter Backup and Restore for more details.
2. Use Add/Remove programs on your primary Tableau Server machine to uninstall Tableau Server.
3. Use Add/Remove programs on your Worker computers to uninstall the worker application.
4. Uninstalling removes the Tableau Server software, but leaves the data, configuration settings and folder structure on the machine.
5. Manually delete the Tableau Server versioned directory. This directory is located under

C:\Program Files\Tableau\Tableau Server

Tableau server default ports

The following table lists the default ports used by Tableau Server.

Port	TCP/UDP	Used By
80	TCP	Gateway
443	TCP	SSL
2233	UDP	Server resource manager UDP port used for communication between Tableau Server processes.
3729	TCP	Tableau Server Setup.
3730–3731	TCP	Tableau worker servers in distributed and highly available Environments (the primary Tableau Server does not listen on these ports).
5000	UDP	Server Worker Manager process (tabadmwrk.exe) Used for auto-discovery of worker servers in a distributed environment.
6379	TCP	Cache Server process (redis-server.exe).
8060	TCP	PostgreSQL database
8061	TCP	PostgreSQL database. Used for **verifying integrity of database** for restoring.
8062	TCP	PostgreSQL database
8080	TCP	Solr, Tomcat HTTP, and Repository processes

8085	TCP	Tomcat HTTP
8250	TCP	Background Tasks
8600	TCP	Application Server process (vizportal.exe). Base port 8600. Consecutive ports after 8600 are used, up to the number of processes.
8700	TCP	Application Server process (vizportal.exe)
8755	TCP	Tableau Administrative process
9100-9199	TCP	VizQL Server process (base port 9100). Consecutive ports after 9100, up to the number of processes, are also used. By default, Tableau Server installs with two VizQL Server processes (ports 9100 and 9101).
9200,9400	TCP	VizQL Server process
9345	TCP	File Store Service
9346	TCP	File Store status service
9700-9899	TCP	Data Server process (base port 9700). Consecutive ports after 9700, up to the number of processes, are also used. By default, Tableau Server installs with two Data Server processes (ports 9700 and 9701).
9800,10000	TCP	Data Server Process
11000	TCP	Search Server

11100	TCP	Search server
12000	TCP	Coordination controller (ZooKeeper) client port
12012	TCP	Cluster Controller process
12013	TCP	Cluster Controller process
13000	TCP	Coordination controller (ZooKeeper) leader port
14000	TCP	Coordination controller (ZooKeeper) leader election port
27000-27009	TCP	Workers and primary server to communicate licensing information in distributed and highly available environments.
	TCP	One additional port is dynamically chosen for workers and the primary server to communicate licensing information in distributed and highly available environments.
27042	TCP	Data Engine process. Tableau Server installs with one Data Engine process. There can be up to two Data Engine processes per node.

3
Tableau Server Workspace

To administer Tableau Server, login to Tableau server URL. Server url will depend on the specific organization but it will be similar to http://Servermachine-name:80. If you have installed a trial version or if the Server is installed on your laptop, you can type Local host and the login screen will appear.

Login with your Administrator credentials, you have setup during installation.

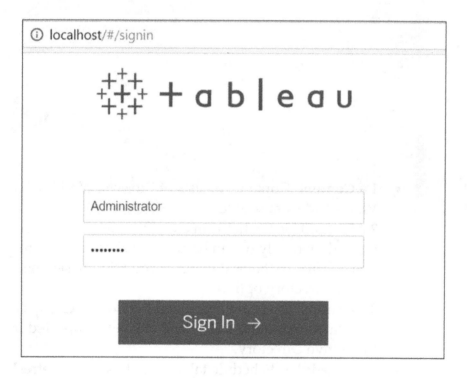

❖ If you are a member of multiple sites, you will be requested to select one site.

Tableau Server Workspace

On successful login, you will enter a workspace like the one below.

This section will give a brief overview of the available tabs. In the later sections, you will get more details on all the tabs.

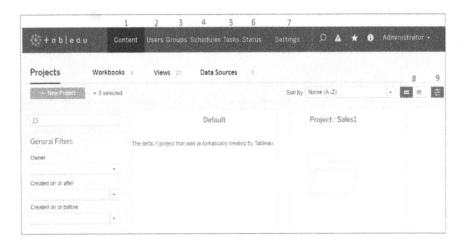

- **1 – Content**. Content consists of Projects, Workbooks, Views and Data sources.
- **2 – Users**. This tab helps in creating users. Users can be created manually or can be added via Active directory or a csv file. In the trial version, you will not see the Active directory option.
- **3 – Groups**. Users are organized in Groups. Groups can be created manually in Tableau or can be imported from the Active Directory.
- **4 – Schedules**. Schedule tab is used to set data refresh and subscription schedule.
- **5 -Tasks**. Runs the schedules.
- **6 – Status**. Status tab provides information about the different services running on the Server. Examples of

- such services are Gateway, Application Server, VizQL and so on.
- **7 – Settings**. This tab contains 3 subtabs
  - General. Specify different configuration settings such as Storage limit for content, Revision history, managing users and so on.
  - Licenses. This tab provides information regarding the licenses owned by the server.
  - Add a Site. This option allows creation of multiple sites.
- **8 – Project display layout**. These provide display options of the Projects. You can display them as thumbnails or list. You can also search and sort your content.
- **9 – Display Filter**. Hide or display filters.

- ❖ Server Administrator has complete access to the Server functionality and can grant permissions to the Site Admins and other users.

Details on Server Tabs

As we learned in the earlier section, server tabs provide different kinds of functionalities that help in managing the resources on the server.

This section will provide a little more detail about the various tabs. Depending on the access, all these tabs may or may not be visible/accessible to the Site Administrator.

Content

Content tab has four sub-tabs
- **Projects**.
  This tab is used to add/modify a **Project**.

  + New Project

A Project is a collection of related Workbooks, Views and Data sources. Projects are related to a specific Site. A Project named **Default** is automatically created with the Server setup. User with Server or Site Administrator privilege can create projects and assign permissions to it. Multiple Projects can be created in a Site.

- **Workbooks.** This tab contains all the published Workbooks. A Workbook is a collection of Views.
- **Views.** This tab contains Views in a Workbook. Views are specific sheets and dashboards in a twb/twbx file.
- **Data Sources.** This tab contains Data Sources published to the server. Data sources can be published directly to the server or as part of the workbook.

Users

Users tab helps in creating new users. These users will be assigned to a **Group** and will be granted different sets of permissions to the **Content** and the Server.

Adding Users

+ Add Users is used to add users in Tableau Server. Users can be added manually, can be uploaded via CSV. Users can also be configured with the Active Directory Server.

- ❖ Active directory is a server for user management. It contains all the users in an organization and the roles assigned to them.
- ❖ Active directory option will not be displayed in trial version of Tableau Server.

To add a user manually, click on **New User**

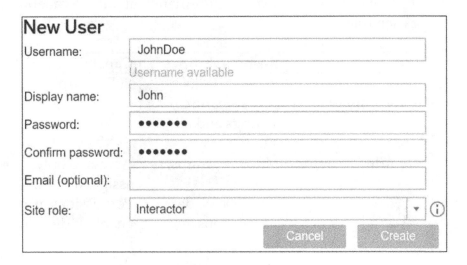

A user can be assigned different Site roles such as

Server Administrator
Site Administrator
Publisher
Interactor
Viewer
Unlicensed
Viewer (can publish)
Unlicensed (can publish)

Site Role

The table below will provide information about the capabilities of each role.

Role	Responsibilities	Capabilities
Server Administrator	Access to all Server features, settings and all sites	Full control.
Site Administrator	Manage groups, projects, workbooks, data connections and Users	Access to only assigned Sites. Permissions are enabled/disabled by the Server Admin.
Publisher	Publish, interact and download workbooks and data sources on the server	Cannot manage other users.
Interactor	Interact with the assigned workbooks, views and Projects.	Cannot publish content to the server.
Viewer	Can only see the assigned views, add and view comments.	Cannot interact with the views like using the filters or sorting.
Unlicensed	Cannot sign-in to the server.	When a User is added beyond the number of licenses permitted, the user is assigned an Unlicensed role.

Viewer (can publish)	Can publish the views	Cannot interact with the views.
Unlicensed (can publish)	Cannot sign-in directly to the Server but can publish views by connecting to the Server from Tableau desktop	

A word about Guest Users

Tableau Server provides a special functionality where an unauthenticated user without a user account on the server can interact with embedded views.

- The Guest user option is available only with the core-based license.
- The Guest user account can be enabled by navigating to Server/Settings/General.

Guest Access

People that are not signed into a Tableau Server account can see views on this site that have guest access permissions.

Guest access is currently disabled for the server. Contact your server administrator.

✓ Enable guest access

- A Guest user cannot browse the Server interface and will not have access to other server functionalities such as users, account settings etc.
- A Guest user cannot publish or own a content.
- A Guest user account is only managed by the Server Administrators and not by Site Administrators.

- A Guest user can have full permissions on Projects, Workbooks and Views. This user is also permitted to export images, view Summary data, view comments, Filter, Full Data, Web Edit, Download (to save a local copy)
- Data source view and download is also permitted.
- A Guest user can also be part of a Group. Group permissions do not apply to Guest user permissions. A Guest user is confined to the permissions directly assigned to him.

Groups
Tableau Server users can be organized in Groups. Groups can be created manually on the Server or imported from the Active directory. Groups can be assigned permissions based on the Project, Workbook, View and data source. A user added to the Tableau Server will belong to a specific Group.

❖ "All Users" group is created by default in all the Sites. Every user added to the Server becomes a member of the **All Users** group automatically. This group cannot be deleted but you can enable/disable permissions to it.

Groups are added by clicking on **New Groups**
In the trial version of Tableau Server, you will not see an option to Add group from the Active directory.
Once the Group is created, Users can be added to it.

Groups 5

		↑ Name	Users
	🔍		
☐	👥 All Users •••		7
☐	👥 Sales •••		0
☐	👥 Sales 1 •••		2
☐	👥 Sales 2 •••		1
☐	👥 Sales 3 •••		1

+ New Group ▼ 0 selected

If licensed version of the Server is used, you can import groups from Active directory. When groups are imported from Active directory, corresponding group in created in Tableau Server with the users in the group.

To delete or rename a Group, click on ... next to the Group name.

❖ If a user already exists in the Tableau server and that user's role gets imported as part of the Active directory group, then the User's Site role will change only if the Active directory group enhances his role with more privileges.

Schedules and Tasks

This tab provides options to setup a new schedule. It provides a list of all the existing schedules, associated tasks, and when they are scheduled to run.

Data extract can be scheduled to run at a specific time.

- To explain **Schedules** and **Tasks**, I have published a data source **Orders (Sample - Superstore)_Extract** on the Server.

- Navigate to Content/Data Sources

- Click on **...** next to the Data source name and select **Refresh Extracts** to schedule a refresh.

- In the next screen, select your schedule by selecting **Schedule a Refresh**.

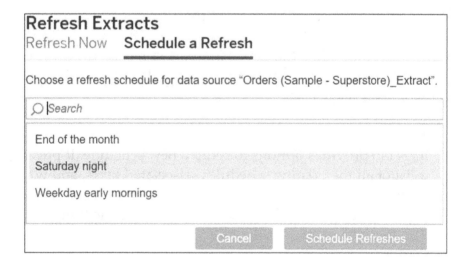

- Now navigate to the **Schedules** tab. In the list of schedules, see the schedule with the task which you created for this data source.

↑ Name		Frequency	Task type	Tasks	Execution	Next run at
📅 End of the month	•••	Monthly	Extract Refresh	0	Parallel	May 31, 2017, 11:00 PM
📅 Monday morning	•••	Weekly	Subscription		Parallel	May 29, 2017, 6:00 AM
📅 Saturday night	•••	Weekly	Extract Refresh	1	Parallel	May 27, 2017, 11:00 PM
📅 Weekday early mornings	•••	Weekly	Extract Refresh	0	Parallel	May 24, 2017, 4:00 AM
📅 Weekday mornings	•••	Weekly	Subscription		Parallel	May 24, 2017, 6:00 AM

- Navigate to Tasks to see the associated Tasks

Extract Refreshes 1   Subscriptions 0

▾ 0 selected

↑ Workbook / Data Source	Refresh type	Schedule
🗄 Orders (Sample - Superstore)_Extract •••	Full refresh	Saturday night – Weekly at 11:00 PM on Saturday

- New schedule can be created by using

New Schedule

Create a schedule users can choose for running extract refreshes or subscriptions.

Name	Hourly Run
Task type	• Extract Refresh ▾
	Subscription
Default priority	50

Tasks are executed in priority order from 1 to 100

Execution ⦿ Parallel: Use all available background processes for this schedule
　　　　　　○ Serial: Limit this schedule to one background process

Frequency ⦿ Hourly　　　　every | 1 hour ▾ |
　　　　　　○ Daily
　　　　　　○ Weekly　　　　from | 12 ▾ | : | 00 ▾ | | AM ▾ |
　　　　　　○ Monthly　　　　to | 12 ▾ | : | 00 ▾ | | AM ▾ |

[Cancel]　[Create]

❖ Task type can be Extract Refresh or Subscription. Extract Refresh is used to refresh data extracts and Subscription works when users Subscribes to a View; he gets an email with the snapshot of the view with the latest data at the scheduled time.

Status

Status tab contains many sub-sections – Process Status, Analysis, Log Files, Rebuild Search Index

Process Status provides the Status of the various processes on the Server.

Process Status
The real-time status of processes running in Tableau Server.

Process	10.45.265.65
Gateway	✓
Application Server	✓
VizQL Server	✓
Cache Server	✓
Search & Browse	✓
Backgrounder	✓
Data Server	✓
Data Engine	✓
File Store	✓
Repository	✓

Refresh Status   ✓ Active ◉ Busy Passive ⚠ Unlicensed ✕ Down Status unavailable

Tableau Server Process Functions

Each process in Tableau server is responsible for a specific task. Some processes run on a single machine, some can be run on multiple machines, in a distributed environment.

Process	Function
Gateway httpd.exe	A webserver component, handles requests to the server from all the clients – Tableau desktop, mobile devices etc.
Application Server Vizportal.exe	Manages the web application, REST API calls, browsing and searching
VizQL Server Vizqlserver.exe	Loads and renders views, computes and executes queries
Cache Server Redis-server.exe	Responsible for Query cache.
Search & Browse	Manages fast search filter, retrieval and

Searchserver.exe	meta content display on the server
Backgrounder Backgrounder.exe	Executes server tasks, including extract refreshes and subscriptions.
Data Server Dataserver.exe	Manages connections to Tableau Server data sources.
Data Engine tdeserver64.exe	Used for storing data extracts and query results.
File Store Filestore.exe	It is installed with the data engine. It automatically replicates extracts across data engine nodes
Repository Progres.exe	Server database, stores workbooks and user metadata.

Analysis

This tab provides the **Analysis** on the usage of the dashboards and other items on the Server. Clicking on each of the link on the left provides more details.

Analysis	
Dashboard	**Analysis**
Traffic to Views	Usage and users for published views.
Traffic to Data Sources	Usage and users for published data sources.
Actions by All Users	Actions for all users.
Actions by Specific User	Actions for a specific user, including items used.
Actions by Recent Users	Recent actions by users, including last action time and idle time.
Background Tasks for Extracts	Completed and pending extract task details.
Background Tasks for Non Extracts	Completed and pending background task details (non-extract).
Stats for Load Times	View load times and performance history.
Stats for Space Usage	Space used by published workbooks and data sources, including extracts and live connections.
Background Task Delays	Difference between scheduled and actual start times of background tasks.
Performance of Views	Overall distribution of view load times and slowest views in a given time period.
Server Disk Space	Current and historical disk space usage, by server node.

Log Files

The Administrator can create and download a snapshot of the Server log files. The zipped snapshot contains a copy of up to seven days of logs from Tableau Server. In a distributed installation, this will contain logs from worker nodes too.

After Log files are downloaded, you can also delete the snapshot.

Date generated	Size	Status
May 24, 2017, 9:08 PM	7.3 MB	Snapshot ready to download.

Generate Snapshot   Download Snapshot   Delete Snapshot

Rebuild Search Index
Rebuild the search Index, if Search is returning incorrect results or if Search option is not been refreshed for a long time

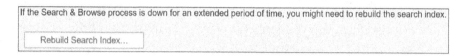

If the Search & Browse process is down for an extended period of time, you might need to rebuild the search index.

Rebuild Search Index...

It is advisable to rebuild the search index after stopping the server. If search index is rebuilt when users are logged in, some of the content may disappear and will appear after the build is complete.

4
Security

To implement security in Tableau server, 4 components should be considered:

Authentication verifies a user's identity on the server.
Authorization deals with how and what the user can access on the Server, after authentication or user credentials have been verified.
Data Security deals with what data the user is authorized to view.
Network Security deals with how Tableau Server connects to different interfaces such as Clients (web browser, Tableau desktop etc.), databases or server components.

Authentication

To access any of the functionality on the Sever, a user account must be present on the server and a site role should be assigned to the user.

- Authentication is a process that allows users to sign in to the Server and perform operations.
- The user is authenticated when he enters his userid and password by accessing Tableau Server url. An unauthenticated user is denied permission.
- User credentials are added to the Server via Server UI, tabcmd commands or using REST API.
- When user credentials are entered in Server, the Tableau Server repository is used to authenticate the user, using Local Authentication methodology.
- If Active Directory is configured to enter the user's credentials, the Active directory is used to authenticate the user.

- Access Permissions on Tableau server are driven by Site roles. Site roles are explained in the previous sections.
- Presence of User account on the server, does not automatically guarantee the access to the data source. For data source access additional configuration is required at the data source level.

- ❖ Authentication methods such as Local Authentication or Active directory are set during the Server installation.

Single sign-on

Tableau server provides different types of Single sign-on (SSO) options.

SSO is very useful in corporate environments. With SSO, the user does not have to sign-in explicitly to the Tableau Server; the credentials used to login into another application/s can be used for Tableau Server authentication. For e.g. if a user is authenticated to login to a corporate network, his same authentication can be used for Tableau Server as well. He does not have to enter his userid and password again to access Tableau Server.

Different types of Single-sign-on mechanism are:
- **SAML.** Security Assertion Markup Language (SAML) is an XML standard that allows secure web domains to exchange user authentication and authorization. It can be configured with Tableau Server to use an External Identity Provider to authenticate Tableau Users. Tableau Server usage of Active directory or local authentication does not matter, as all user authentications are performed outside Tableau.
- **Kerberos.** Kerberos is a computer network authentication mechanism. It authenticates computers via exchange of tickets. Kerberos works when the Tableau Server is configured with Active directory.

- **Trusted Authentication.** Trusted authentication comes into play when Tableau views are embedded into webpages. It allows the user account to be authenticated in the webpage or web application so that user is not prompted when he accesses Tableau views. Trusted authentication is a mechanism that establishes trusted relationship between Tableau Server and webserver/s. When Tableau server receives requests from these trusted webservers, it assumes that all necessary authentication is handled by the webserver.

How Trusted Authentication Works

1. A User visits the webpage with the embedded Tableau Server view.
   a. The webpage sends a **GET** request to the web server for the HTML for that page.
   b. The web server sends a POST request to the trusted Tableau Server. The POST request will have a username parameter. This username is a licensed Tableau Server User. If the user and view are associated to a site, then target_site parameter should be included.
2. IP address or host name of the source web server is verified by the Tableau Server. A unique ticket is created if the webserver is listed as a trusted host.
   The issued Ticket should be redeemed within three minutes. Tableau Server responds to the POST request with this ticket.
3. Using the ticket, the web server creates a URL for the view and inserts it into the HTML of the webpage. The web server passes the HTML back to the client's web browser.
4. The client web browser sends a GET request to the Tableau Server that includes the URL with the ticket.

5. Tableau Server redeems the ticket, creates a session, allows the user to login, removes the ticket from the URL, and then sends the final URL for the embedded view to the client.

Authorization

Authorization deals with the permissions each user is granted on the Tableau Server after authentication is performed. Authorization allows users to perform operations on the Tableau server based on the Site role and associated permissions.

Authorization is performed by the use of:

- **Site Roles**. Site roles are a set of permissions that are assigned to a user. Each role is a collection of capabilities that, a user can have on the Server.
- **Permissions**. Permissions determine if the user can perform specific actions on a specific content element on the Server.

  Permissions are specific to content elements i.e. they are assigned to Projects, Workbooks, Views and Data sources. In order for a user to work on a content element, the user or the user group must be explicitly assigned to the content element.

  The content owner has the permission to work on his content. For e.g. if you publish a workbook or data source to the Server, you are the owner of this workbook or the data source. You can view, interact, or delete the workbook or data source which you owned.

  User permissions can be granted in the Tableau Desktop while publishing a content such as Workbook

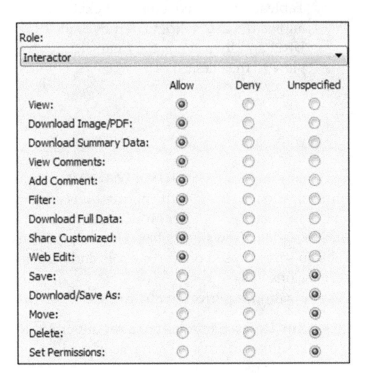

Or at the Server level

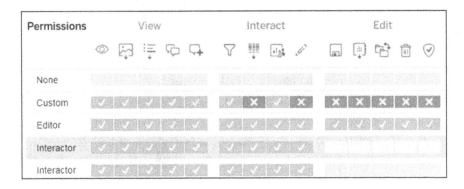

Data Security

In Tableau, you have different ways to setup which user can see which data. For data sources, that connect to live databases, when users click on the published views, you can set whether the user would be prompted to enter database passwords. The following options can be followed for providing Data Security:

- **Database login account**. You can setup a database login password to connect to the live source data. Create a view using this data source and publish the view using Tableau desktop. When a user clicks on the view, on the Tableau Server, he will be prompted to enter his credentials

To open this view, you must sign in to the database that the view uses.

Username

Password

☐ Remember my password until I sign out

Sign In

Connection Type: Access
Authentication: Workgroup Security

- **Authentication mode**. When a data source or a view is published, an authentication mode can be selected that depends on how the user can access the data source
  - By using his credentials
  - By embedded credentials. The Publisher can embed database credentials.
  - Server Run as account

- **User filters.** Provide user filters in the Tableau desktop for row level data security. By default, a user who has access to the view, can see all the data in the view. This behaviour can be altered by creating user filter that will restrict the user to view only permitted data.
- ❖ User filters are created in Tableau Desktop. From the main menu, navigate to Server/Create User filter.

Network Security

Tableau Server has three network interfaces:

- **Client to Tableau Server.** A Tableau Server can be accessed from different clients, web browser, Tableau desktop, a device running Tableau mobile or tabcmd utility. By default, all communications use HTTP protocol, Tableau recommends HTTPS for all the communications.
- **Tableau Server to database.** Dynamic connections to databases are made to process result sets and refresh extracts. Tableau uses native drivers to connect to databases whenever possible. It depends on generic ODBC adapter when native drivers are unavailable.
- **Server component/s Communication.** This comes into picture when the Tableau Server is installed in a distributed environment.
  Trust and Transmission are two aspects of communication between the server and the components. Trust is established by a whitelist/approved IP address, port, and protocol. If any of these are invalid, the request is ignored.
  The transmission of all internal communication is performed via HTTP.
  Credentials for external data sources are stored encrypted on Tableau Server internal database. When a process uses these credentials to query the external data source, the process retrieves the encrypted credentials from the internal database and decrypts them in process.

5
Managing Sites

In Tableau Server, Site is a logical space that separates content, data and users from other Sites on the Server.

- Tableau Server permits multi-tenancy by allowing the creation of multiple sites on the server for different groups of users and content.
- When the Tableau server is configured, a default site is automatically created.
- Tableau server Administrator can create multiple sites and create users for these sites. If a user is assigned to multiple Sites, he/she will see an option to select a Site.

Select a Site
Search for a site
Default
Sales

- The primary objective of Site is data isolation.
- Users assigned to a specific site, can view their assigned Site/s and contents on that Site. Server Administrator can see all the Sites.
- Site has its own Users, Groups, Projects, Workbooks, Views and data sources.
- Tableau Server content is always administered per site basis. A default site is always present with initial setup. Even if no other site is present, default site is always present.

- User license is at the Server level. A user can be a member of different sites. He does not need a license for each site.
- Server Administrator can set the limit to the storage space used by the site. Select a site and navigate to Settings.

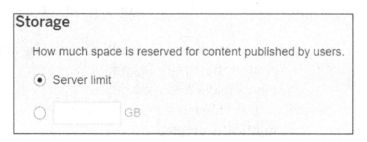

- Server Administrator can limit the number of users permitted per site. Only licensed users are counted; Server administrators and unlicensed users are not counted. Select a site and navigate to Settings.

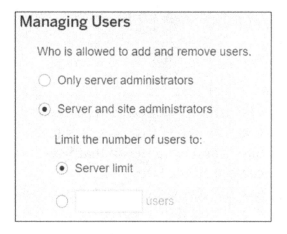

A word about default Site

When the Tableau server is installed and configured, a Site named **Default** is automatically created.

The Default site is different than any other sites created by the Server Administrator.

- It can be renamed but can never be deleted
- It stores the Tableau server samples and data connections. You receive these samples and data connections, with Tableau Server installation.
- The URL for the default site does not mention the Site name. For example, if you click on a view on a default Site, the URL will appear as

http://localhost/#/views/SalesDashboard-
1/Db_SalesMap?:iid=2

If a view is clicked on the Site **Sales**, the URL will appear as

http://localhost/#/site/**Sales**/views/SalesByRegions/Map
s?:iid=1

Server Administrator vs Site Administrator

Following table lists the differences between Server Administrator and Site Administrator roles and responsibilities:

Server Administrator	Site Administrator
Responsible for the entire Server including all the Sites	Responsible for only the assigned Site/s
Can create new Sites	Cannot create new Sites
Install, upgrade and configure the services that run on Tableau Server, back it up, and perform other tasks that pertain to running Tableau Server as a whole.	Manage groups, projects, workbooks, and data connections. Can also schedule data refreshes.
Creates and manages users. Grants permissions to the Site Admins to create users	Limited by the permissions provided by the Server Admin. Cannot create users if permission is not granted.
Can specify the "limit the number of users to" assigned to the site. Only licensed users are counted.	Number of users to the site is limited by the setting configured by the Server Admin. Cannot modify this setting.

Creating a New Site

The Server Admin can create a new site by navigating to **Settings** tab. Click on **Add a Site** and select

Specify the **Name** of the Site, **Storage** and **History** settings.

Server Admin can specify who can **Manage the users** and number of users allowed on the Site.

Web Authoring setting will ensure that the user can only view the published views or he can also edit them in the Server web editing environment.

Workbook Performance Metrics, allows Site admins to collect metrics on workbook performance.

Managing Users
Who is allowed to add and remove users.

- ○ Only server administrators
- ● Server and site administrators

    Limit the number of users to:

    - ● Server limit
    - ○ [ ] users

Web Authoring

Users with the appropriate permissions can edit workbooks in their browser.

- ☑ Allow users to use web authoring

Workbook Performance Metrics

Record performance information about key events as users interact with workbooks. View performance metrics in a workbook that Tableau creates automatically.

- ☐ Record workbook performance metrics

Setting for Offline access and Email notification can also be specified.

Offline Favorites for Tableau Mobile

Let users access favorite workbooks and views, even if they're disconnected from the server.

- ☑ Enable offline favorites

Email Notification

Email notification lets data source and workbook owners know when and why Tableau could not complete a scheduled refresh.

- ☑ Send email to data source and workbook owners when scheduled refreshes fail

---

Activate, Suspend or Delete a Site

Server Administrators can modify a site status by activating, suspending or deleting a Site.

1. Login to Tableau Server. Click on Manage All Sites.

2. Click on ... next to the site you want to modify

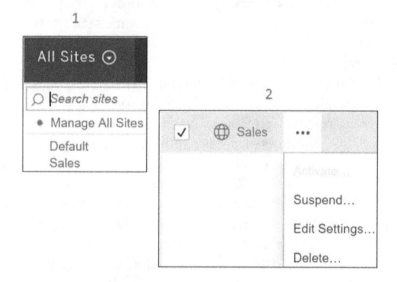

Add Users to the Site
The Site admin, having the privilege to create users, will create users in the same fashion like Server Admins i.e. by adding them manually, by configuring the Active directory or by csv upload.

Importing and Exporting a Site

A site can be created on the Tableau Server by - exporting an existing Site to a file and importing the file into a new Site. The exported site is referred as **Source Site** and the Site into which import occurs is called a **Target site**.
When a site is imported, all of the source site's resources viz. Projects, Groups, Workbooks, Data sources, users will come with it. It also includes all the site-specific settings from the source site.

Plan for Exporting and Importing a site
- Delete unused items from the source site.
- Create user accounts on the target server.
    - When a site is exported/imported on the same server, all user accounts already exist on the server. If the site is exported from a different Tableau Server, user accounts must be created on the target server before the import process.
- Check the user authentication method.
- Configure the target site to deliver subscriptions
- Create or identify the target site. Before import process triggers, a target site should already be identified. With
- the import process, the target site is overridden with the source site. An empty site is recommended.
- Locate Site IDs. The export/import process commands using Site IDs as parameters. A site ID uniquely identifies a site on the server. On the Server Url, site ID is displayed after **#**.

❖ If the server contains no additional sites, then default site is used. The Default site does not have a site ID but double quotation marks with no space is used as a site ID "".

Exporting a Site

Export/Import process can be run without stopping the server. The Exported site will be locked during the process.

Execute **tabadmin exportsite** command to export a site.

Exercise

1. Launch command prompt as an administrator and type

Cd C:\Program Files\Tableau\Tableau Server\10.2\bin

2. Use the command, tabadmin exportsite
   In this example, site Sales is exported and saved in Export_Sales.zip

tabadmin exportsite Sales --file C:\ Export_Sales.zip

```
C:\Program Files\Tableau\Tableau Server\10.2\bin>tabadmin exportsite Sales --file C:\Export_Sales.zip
 -- Locked site Sales
===== Exporting site Sales
===== The site has been exported to C:\Export_Sales.zip
 -- Unlocked site Sales
```

Importing a Site

To import a site, identify a site/target site where this import will occur. Create a new site, if site does not exist.

Importing a site is a three-step process.

1. Run the tabadmin importsite command to generate the files that will be imported.
2. Verify files that show how the site will be imported.
3. Run the tabadmin importsite_verified command to finish the import.

Exercise

1. For this exercise, create a new site NewSales on the Tableau Server. Refer Creating a New Site in the previous section.
2. Invoke command prompt as an administrator and navigate to the bin directory on Tableau Server.

Cd C:\Program Files\Tableau\Tableau Server\10.2\bin

3. Use the command, tabadmin importsite <site ID> --file
   <filename or path>
   where <site ID> is the target site and <filename or path>
   is the path of the exported site.

| tabadmin importsite NewSales --file C:\ Export_Sales.zip |

```
C:\Program Files\Tableau\Tableau Server\10.2\bin>tabadmin importsite NewSales --file C:\Export_Sales.zip
===== Importing site NewSales
  -- Migrations already up to date.
===== Please follow the steps to finish the import:
=====   1) Verify the mapping files under C:\ProgramData\Tableau\Tableau Server\data\tabsvc\temp\import_5329a36c_2017062
3222501120\mappings
=====   2) Run the command: 'tabadmin importsite_verified "NewSales" --importjobdir "C:\ProgramData\Tableau\Tableau Serv
er\data\tabsvc\temp\import_5329a36c_20170623222501120"'
```

Verify the Site Mappings

After importsite command is successfully run, it generates
several mapping files. These mapping files are located under

| C:\ProgramData\Tableau\Tableau
Server\data\tabsvc\temp\import_5329a36c_20170623222501120 |

These mapping files show how the Site's content will be
mapped once the import is complete.
You need to open each folder/file under this path and fix
errors, if any.
The files and folders under this path will appear like:

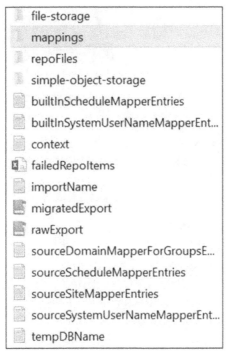

Once you have verified and fixed mapping files manually, run the importsite_verified command to complete the import process.

Syntax

tabadmin importsite_verified <site ID> --importjobdir <PATH>

where <site ID> is the target site, path is the path of the mapping files.

> tabadmin importsite_verified NewSales --importjobdir
> "C:\ProgramData\Tableau\Tableau
> Server\data\tabsvc\temp\import_5329a36c_20170623222501120"

```
C:\Program Files\Tableau\Tableau Server\10.2\bin>tabadmin importsite_verified NewSales --importjobdir "C:\ProgramData\Ta
bleau\Tableau Server\data\tabsvc\temp\import_5329a36c_20170623222501120"
    -- Locked site NewSales
===== Importing site NewSales
===== site NewSales successfully imported
    -- Unlocked site NewSales
```

Now login to your server, you can see NewSales site.

Maintaining revision history

Server Administrators can permit Sites to keep revision history of the workbooks and data sources. You can keep as many versions as needed, default setting is 25. When not required, revisions can also be deleted.

To enable revision history,

1. Login as Server Administrator. If multiple sites are available, select a Site, where revision history is needed.
2. Navigate to Settings, **Revision History**.

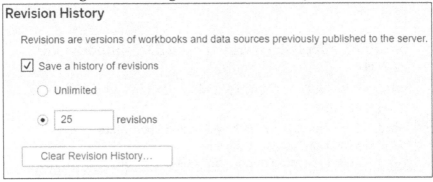

To access revision history, a user must have a Site role of a Publisher.

This user should also have permissions on Workbooks to View, Save, and Download Workbook/Save As.

Permissions on Data source/s should be View, Save, and Download Data Source.

6
Branding

Branding involves customizing the look and feel of your Tableau server so that it represents your organization.

The following types of customizations can be done
- Change the Tableau server name that appears in the browser tab, tooltips, and messages.
- Replace the Tableau logo with your organization's logo
- Manage the language used for the server UI (user interface) and the locale used for views.
- Use custom fonts on Tableau Server and client computers that connect to Tableau Server.
- Add images for Projects in thumbnail view.

- ❖ Branding is available only at the Server level. Till the present version, Site branding options are not available in Tableau.

Add customized name or logo
As a first step in the branding process, change the Tableau Server look and feel by providing your own Custom Server name and logo.

The Custom name will appear on the browser tab and in the tooltip, when users hover over the custom logo in the upper left corner of the main page. The custom logo will appear on the sign-in page, the server page header and in web authoring pages.
- ❖ Not all references to Tableau Server can be changed. The logo on the browser window and the phrase "Tableau Server" in the copyright notice cannot be changed.

Changing the Server name

As a first step in the branding process, change the name of the Tableau Server as it appears on the **browser** tab and **tool tip**. Tableau Server name is changed using the **tabadmin** commands.

By default, the browser tab appears as below in the Server UI

Exercise

1. Launch command prompt, as an administrator
    To launch the command prompt as administrator in windows 10, right click on start programs icon and select Command Prompt (Admin)

2. Type the following,

```
cd "C:\Program Files\Tableau\Tableau Server\10.2\bin"
```

3. Type the following command. **customize name** will change the default "Tableau Server" to new name "OCA"

```
tabadmin customize name "OCA"
```

4. Restart the server so that the changes can take effect.

```
tabadmin restart
```

With all the commands, the Command prompt window will appear like

```
C:\WINDOWS\system32>cd "C:\Program Files\Tableau\Tableau Server\10.2\bin"

C:\Program Files\Tableau\Tableau Server\10.2\bin>tabadmin customize name "OCA"

C:\Program Files\Tableau\Tableau Server\10.2\bin>tabadmin restart
===== Stopping service...
  -- Service stopped successfully
===== Starting service...
  -- Service was started successfully
```

After the above changes, your browser tab will look like the one below, with new custom name OCA and tool tip.

Changing the Logo

On the Tableau Sever UI, different Tableau logos appear at different places,

Sign_in_logo. Appears when the sign-in window is displayed.

Header_logo. Appears in the upper left when the user is signed in and the main content page is displayed.

Smalllogo. Appears in the upper left when a view is being edited for web authoring.

❖ The image files used should be in GIF, JPEG, or PNG format.

The **sign_in_logo** image can be a maximum of 3000 by 3000 pixels.

The **header_logo** image can be up to 160 by 160 pixels, but not smaller than 32 by 32 pixels. For best results use an image that is 125 by 35 pixels. If the image is larger than 160 by 160 pixels, it is clipped.

The smalllogo image can be up to 32 by 32 pixels. For best results use an image that is 32 by 32 pixels.

If the images are not displayed in the correct size, they can be resized.

Changing the sign_in logo

By default, the Sign_in page with sign_in_logo appears with the Tableau logo, see below

The Tableau logo on this page can be replaced with the customized logo

Exercise

1. Launch command prompt, as an administrator and type the following

   ```
   cd "C:\Program Files\Tableau\Tableau Server\10.2\bin"
   ```

2. Use **customize sign_in_logo** to change the signin logo

   ```
   tabadmin customize sign_in_logo
   "C:\TableauBranding\OCA_logo_Signin.jpg"
   ```

   where C:\TableauBranding\OCA_logo_Signin.jpg is the path and file name of customized logo created for this exercise.

3. Restart the server so that changes can take effect. Type

   ```
   tabadmin restart
   ```

After executing these steps, the sign-in logo will be changed to reflect customized logo

Changing the header_logo
By default, the Tableau header_logo appears once the user is on the content page.

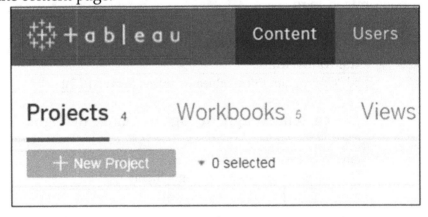

This logo can also be replaced by the customized logo

Exercise

1. Launch command prompt, as an administrator and type the following

cd "C:\Program Files\Tableau\Tableau Server\10.2\bin"

2. Type **customize header_logo** command to change the header logo

tabadmin customize header_logo "C:\TableauBranding\OCA_logo_Header.jpg"

   where C:\TableauBranding\OCA_logo_Header.jpg is the path and file name of the customized logo created for this exercise.

3. Restart the server so that changes can take effect. Type

tabadmin restart

After this change, the header logo will appear like the one below,

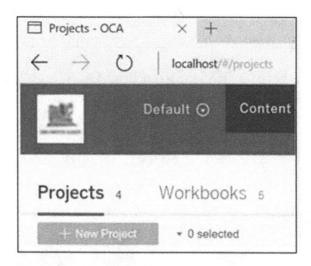

Changing the smalllogo

By default, Tableau smalllogo appears in the upper left when a view is being edited for web authoring.

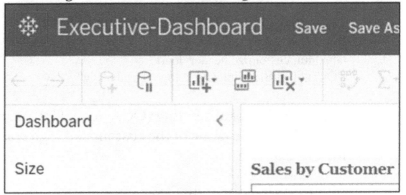

Exercise
1. Launch command prompt, as an administrator and type the following

   ```
   cd "C:\Program Files\Tableau\Tableau Server\10.2\bin"
   ```

2. Type **customize smalllogo** command to change the small logo

   ```
   tabadmin customize smalllogo
   "C:\TableauBranding\OCA_logo_SmallLogo.jpg"
   ```

   where C:\TableauBranding\OCA_logo_SmallLogo.jpg is the path and file name of the customized logo created for this exercise.

3. Restart the server so that changes can take effect. Type

   ```
   tabadmin restart
   ```

After following the above steps, the small logo will appear

Restoring to default header logo

In case, you want to restore to the original logo, use

```
tabadmin customize parameter -d
```

where parameter is the name, logo, header_logo, sign_in_logo, or smalllogo.

If by mistake, you upload an incorrect logo as the Header_logo, you can restore the original logo as follows:

Exercise

1. Launch command prompt, as an administrator and type the following

```
cd "C:\Program Files\Tableau\Tableau Server\10.2\bin"
```

2. Use the tabadmin command

```
tabadmin customize header_logo -d
```

3. Restart the server so that changes can take place effect.

```
tabadmin restart
```

Changing the colors on Tableau Server

You can change the colors on Tableau Server UI according to your corporate requirements. These changes can be done by making changes to the files under

C:\Program Files\Tableau\Tableau Server\10.2\vizportalclient\public

❖ A lot of changes can be performed using the files under this location; in this section, you will learn how to change the background color of the top banner.

Changing the background Color of the banner

As part of the branding, you may want to change the color of the Tableau Server banner to your corporate colors.
This is done by modifying the Tableau Sever files.
These files are located in your Tableau Server directory

C:\Program Files\Tableau\Tableau Server\10.2\vizportalclient\public

How to change the background color of the top banner

To change the background color of the top banner,
You need to modify:
- Vizportal.css
- Vizportal.js
- Vizportal.min.js

For each of these files, you also need to create a **.gz** version (compressed version created using 7-Zip) Tableau uses these files in displaying colors and other settings.

❖ Modification to these files are not supported by Tableau, make sure to take backups to these files before making any changes.

Exercise

In this exercise, we will change the top blue color banner of the Tableau Server.

To replace Tableau's color, select color RGB(204,133,166) or #CC85A6. You can also choose any other color of your choice.

1. On your Tableau server installation directory, navigate to

C:\Program Files\Tableau\Tableau Server\10.2\vizportalclient\public

2. Open **vizportal.css**. Use Notepad ++ to edit this file.
   a. Search for **.tb-top-bar** in the script and change the background color to the required color.
   b. Search for **.tb-top-bar-toggle** in the script and change the background color to the required color
   c. Save the file.
3. Open **vizportal.js**. Use Notepad ++ to edit this file.
   a. Search for **ServerBlue** and change the RGB values.
   b. Search for **HeaderStyles.HeaderBackgroundColor** and change the RGB values.
   c. Save the file
4. Open **vizportal.min.js**. Use Notepad ++ to edit this file.
   a. Search for **ServerBlue** and change the RGB values.
   b. Search for **e.HeaderBackgroundColor** and change the RGB values.
   c. Save the file
5. Take a backup of the existing .gz files for the above three files. Create new .gz files for each of these files.
6. Launch command prompt as Admin and type

cd "C:\Program Files\Tableau\Tableau Server\10.2\bin"

7. Restart the server by typing

tabadmin restart

- ❖ .gz files are compressed files and are created using 7-Zip. If you don't have 7-Zip you can always download.

- ❖ In case your changes do not reflect, clear the browser cache and also the cache of your webserver. You can also try a different browser.

Language and Locale

Internationalization and localization are ways to present your application in different languages and regions. These settings can affect the visualization application in terms of the language, date format and currency.

Tableau desktop and Tableau server can be localized to support users in different countries and locale.

Locale configuration setting is independent of language and controls how numbers, dates and times are displayed in a specific region.

Language setting controls the language which gets displayed on a text in your visualization.

- ❖ Tableau supports Unicode/double byte character sets, which helps in displaying any language.

Language and Locale Setting - Desktop

In the Tableau deskop, **Language** setting can be configured for each workbook.

To modify the Language setting, navigate to **main menu-Help/Choose Language**.

Tableau desktop should be restarted after the change.

Locale Setting in Tableau desktop is done from the File menu.

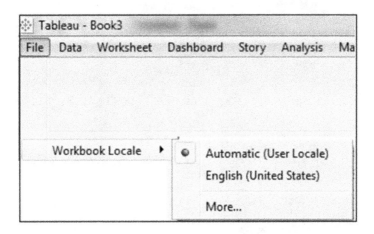

If Automatic (User Locale) is selected, Windows Operating System Locale and Tableau Desktop Language is checked to determine the locale of the workbook.

If any value other than Automatic (User Locale) is selected for the Workbook Locale, then that selection will drive all localization for the workbook.

Change Language and Locale in the workbook
Exercise
1. Launch Tableau desktop and connect to Tableau provided data source **Sample-Super Store.xls** or some other data source of your choice.
2. Create a sheet by using Region as dimension and Profit, Quantity and Sales from the measures

By default, English Language and Automatic (User Locale) the visualization will look like the following

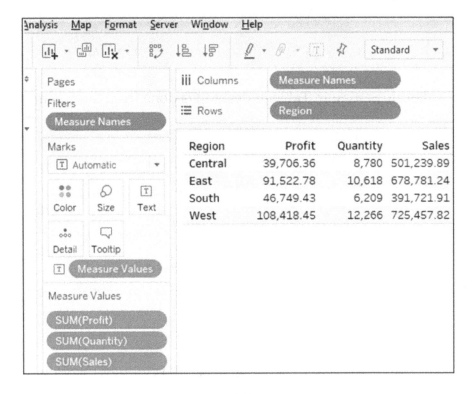

3. Now, change language to Francias from Menu - **Help/Choose Language**.

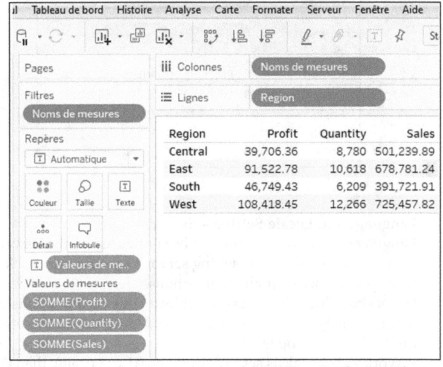

You will notice that Language in the Tableau Desktop UI has changed but the number formatting follows the User's windows Operating System i.e. English.

4. Now, navigate to the File menu and change the **Workbook Locale** to francias (France)

Notice that everything else remains the same as the above screen-shot in French but the number format changes this time to reflect the France Locale. Commas have appeared in place of decimals.

| iii Colonnes | Noms de mesures | | |
| ::: Lignes | Region | | |

Region	Profit	Quantity	Sales
Central	39 706,36	8 780	501 239,89
East	91 522,78	10 618	678 781,24
South	46 749,43	6 209	391 721,91
West	108 418,45	12 266	725 457,82

Language and Locale Setting – Server

Language and Locale setting can be configured on the Server too but Workbook Locale setting set for a specific workbook takes precedence over all other options.

If workbook locale is set using Tableau Desktop and published to a Tableau Server, it will be displayed using the locale set at the Tableau desktop level.

If Workbook Locale is set to Automatic (User Locale), then the other settings will come into action.

Language and Locale settings inside Tableau Server

- Default language and locale – On Tableau Server UI, available on the **Settings** page, select **Manage All Sites** from the site drop down and navigate to **Settings**.
- Language and locale: set by individual user through the **User Preferences** on User account page.

User Preferences page settings supersedes the Language and Locale configurations done by the Administrator.

The default language for Tableau Server is determined during installation and Setup. If the server machine is configured for a language Tableau Server supports, Tableau Server installs that language as its default. If an unsupported language is used, Tableau Server installs English as its default language.

How Language and Locale is implemented on the Server
User's web browser also determines how Language and locale are displayed.

If a user has not defined a Language setting on his User Account page, and the web browser language is different from the Tableau server language, web browser language will take precedence as long as it uses one of the server supported languages.

Example,
The Tableau Server has a setting of English as the Language for all users and a Server user John, does not have a language specified on his Tableau Server User Account page. If John's browser uses Francias (France) for its language/locale, the Server UI will display in French and all France locale for numbers and currency will be displayed.

If John modifies his User account page and selects Espanol as the language, the server UI, numbers and currency will be displayed in Espanol. The User account setting will take precedence over Server and Browser language and locale.

❖ The Tableau Desktop- workbook locale setting takes precedence over all the settings.

7
Performance and Monitoring

An efficiently performing Server is a key for success in any visualization application.

There are several key variables that affect the Server performance and a combination of all these variables will help in improving the performance.

Guidelines for better Performance

- **Requirements**. Ensure all hardware and software requirements are met for the installation of Tableau server.
- **64-bit version**. In corporate environments always use 64-bit operating system and 64-bit version of the Tableau Server. Tableau 10 comes in only in 64-bit but earlier versions were available in both 32-bit and 64-bit.
- **Cores and Memory**. Adding more cores and RAM to your system will help, regardless of Tableau server single-machine installation or a distributed environment.
- **Data refresh schedule**. Big Data refreshes should be scheduled in the off-peak hours.
- **VizQL session timeout limit**. By default, VizQL session timeout limit is 30 minutes, set this limit to a lower value so that VizQL session does not consume the memory when idle. This can be done using the tabadmin commands.
- **VizQL clear Session**. VizQL sessions consume lot of memory even when the user is navigated away from the view. The Administrator can set the configuration, to end the session when the user has navigated away.

This can be done by setting *vizqlserver.clear_session_on_unload to true*. This can be done using the tabadmin commands.

- **Caching**. Configure the cache setting to *Refresh less often*. This setting is available on the **Data Connections** tab on Tableau Server configuration.
- **Server Process Settings**. Tableau server is divided under several different server processes. These server processes configurations can be modified to improve the performance.
- **Scale up**. Depending on the Server usage, you can scale up your Tableau Server installation by adding more worker nodes (distributed installation). The decision to add more nodes will usually depend on concurrent usage of the Sever, heavy use of extracts and fail over.
- **Optimize workbooks and extracts**. Use Tableau desktop to optimize your workbooks and extracts.

Adding more resources to the Server

Consider adding more resources to the server for better performance. The decision to scale up will depend on :

- Number of concurrent users. If at any given time, the number of concurrent users is greater than 100, adding more VizQL processes and more workers should be considered.
- Big extracts can severely impact the performance of the Server. If the Site depends on many big and small extracts, configure data engine process on a separate machine.
- If your business data needs frequent data extracts then additional background process should be considered.

Configuring the Server Processes

Configuration of the Server process is done through "Tableau Server Configuration". This utility will be available on the machine where the Tableau Server is installed.

Configuration of the Server processes can be modified to achieve better performance.

For a Single-machine installation or primary Tableau Server installation, the processes will appear as

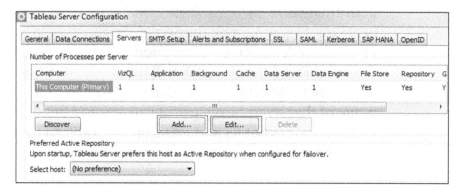

Click on **Edit** to add or remove the number of processes. Additional worker nodes can be added by clicking on the **Add**.

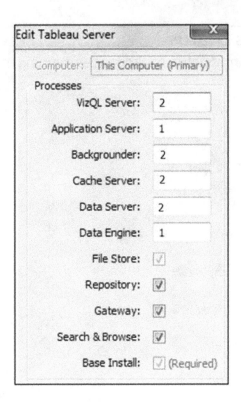

Single Machine Configuration

For a single machine with minimum Hardware requirements for the Tableau server, the recommended configuration is

2 VizQL server processes, 2 cache server processes, and 2 data server processes.

These processes are displayed on the Tableau Server UI under the status tab.

Process Status

The real-time status of processes running in Tableau Server.

Process	Server-3KLT9bD	
Gateway	✓	
Application Server	✓	
VizQL Server	✓	✓
Cache Server	✓	✓
Search & Browse	✓	
Backgrounder	✓	✓
Data Server	✓	✓
Data Engine	✓	
File Store	✓	
Repository	✓	

❖ On a node, cache server process should run for every VizQL server process.

❖ The least number of background processes to run, can be calculated as machine's total number of cores divided by 4.

❖ Data refreshes should be scheduled for off-peak times.

How views are rendered in Tableau

Views or visualizations are created using Tableau desktop and published on the Server. Users access the views on the server via Server url. These views are extracted, interpreted and then rendered on the client web browser.

The Tableau server can perform this action in the client web browser or the server. Depending on the complexity of the view, and the device used to the access the view, the Tableau Server can decide whether to perform Server-side rendering or client-side.

By default, Tableau Server performs Client-side rendering.

	Server rendering	Client rendering
Simple view		✓
Complex view	✓	
Image files		✓
Images created by using data elements	✓	
View opened on PC		✓
View opened on Tablet	✓	
Use of Polygons, Custom Shapes, Page history	✓	

The Tableau Server automatically handles Server or client rendering by using the **Threshold Calculation** to calculate the complexity of the view.

The Threshold calculation as done by Tableau server:

view complexity = (# of marks) + 3(# of headers) + 3(# of annotations) + 3(# of reference lines) + 6(# of unique custom shapes)

If the complexity value > 100 (for PCs) or > 20 (for tablet browsers), the view will be rendered on the server.

Performance Recording

Performance Recording feature is available on Tableau desktop and Tableau Server. It enables you to record performance information about key elements as the user interacts with the workbooks.

Once performance recording is completed, performance metrics are viewed in a "Performance workbook" that Tableau creates automatically.

The Performance recording is created and viewed differently in Tableau Desktop and Tableau Server but the resulting Performance workbooks have the same format in both the cases.

Performance workbooks are used to analyze different performance issues pertaining to different events that affect performance. These events are

- Query execution
- Geocoding
- Connections to data sources
- Layout computations
- Extract generation
- Data Blending
- Server Blending

Enabling Performance Recording for a Site
Server Administrator can configure performance recording for a Site.
Exercise
1. Login as Server Administrator.
2. Navigate to the Site where you want to configure the performance recording. Performance setting can also be set for the default site.

3. Navigate to **Settings**. Under **Workbook Performance Settings**, check **Record workbook performance metrics**.

Workbook Performance Metrics

Record performance information about key events as users interact with workbooks. View performance metrics in a workbook that Tableau creates automatically.

☑ Record workbook performance metrics

---

4. Click save

Start Performance recording for a view
Exercise

1. Navigate to **Content**. Click on the view for which you want to record performance.
   Once the view is open, check the url, Tableau Server appends **iid=<n>** at the end of the url. This is a session id. In this example, it will appear as

   http://localhost/#/views/SalesDashboard-1/Db_SalesMap?:iid=2

2. In the url, before the session id **iid<n>** type **:record_performance=yes&**

   http://localhost/#/views/SalesDashboard-1/Db_SalesMap?:record_performance=yes&:iid=2

3. Press enter or f5 to refresh the url. This will display a new tab **Performance** in the tool bar. This shows that the performance recording has started.

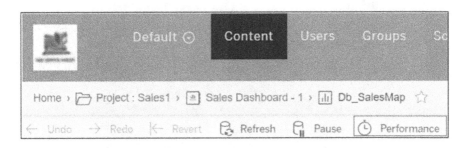

4. Click on **Performance** to open the performance workbook. This workbook is automatically created by Tableau Server. The Performance workbook will update as you work with the view.

❖ The Performance workbook is a Tableau Server generated dashboard and contains 3 sheets viz. Timeline, Events and Query.

Monitoring Sever for Performance

The Tableau Server is monitored to collect and analyze data for performance.

The data that is analysed falls under 3 categories
- Resource usage. How Tableau Server uses hardware components.
- Session and Load time. Time taken to load and interact with the views.
- Background Task. Time taken to execute background tasks such as extract refresh etc.

Administrative Views

The Tableau Server generates Administrative views to help monitoring the health of the Server.
Site Administrators can see the Administrative views for their Site and Server Administrators can see the views for the selected site.

1. Login to Tableau Server as Server Administrator and click on **Status**.
2. Tableau Server provides the following administrative views

Analysis
Dashboards that monitor site activity.

Dashboard	Analysis
Traffic to Views	Usage and users for published views.
Traffic to Data Sources	Usage and users for published data sources.
Actions by All Users	Actions for all users.
Actions by Specific User	Actions for a specific user, including items used.
Actions by Recent Users	Recent actions by users, including last action time and idle time.
Background Tasks for Extracts	Completed and pending extract task details.
Background Tasks for Non Extracts	Completed and pending background task details (non-extract).
Stats for Load Times	View load times and performance history.
Stats for Space Usage	Space used by published workbooks and data sources, including extracts and live connections.

- **Traffic to Views**

Traffic to Views, provides information on how much user traffic is generated by the view. This view can be filtered by – View, Workbook, Time Range and Min View Count
The sheets in this View/dashboard are:
- o What is the View Count by Project?
- o What is the Total View Count by Day?
- o What is the Total View Count by Time?
- o What Views Are Seen the Most? (Views seen >= Min View Count)
- o Who Accesses Views Most Often? (Views seen >= Min View Count)

- **Traffic to Data Sources**

This view provides information on the usage of different Data Sources. The view can be filtered by Data Source name, Actions taken on the data source, Time range and Min interactions
The sheets in this View/dashboard are:
- o What is the Data Source Usage by Project?
- o What is the Total Data Source Usage by Day?
- o What Data Sources Are Used Most? (Data sources used >= Min Interactions)
- o Who uses the Data Sources Most Often? (Data sources used >= Min Interactions)

- **Actions by All Users**

This view provides information on Actions taken by all the users on a Site. The view can be filtered by Action and Time Range. Action relates to the Actions taken by the users i.e. Access View, Download Data Source, Login, download workbook and so on.

There is only one sheets in this View:
   - What Actions are the Users Taking?

- **Actions by Specific Users**

This view gives details about the actions taken by specific users on the Server. The view can be filtered by User name, Actions and Time Range.

The sheets in this View/dashboard are:
   - What Actions is a specific user taking on this Site?
   - What items are used?
      - This gives the Item name i.e. the specific Server resource such as View or data source and Action performed on it.

- **Actions by Recent Users**

This view displays which users are currently active and what Actions are performed by these users. This view is helpful when the Administrator is planning some maintenance activity and wants to see the active users and their activity on the Server.

The sheets in this View/dashboard are :
   - Who was most recently active ?
   - What Actions were Recently Performed?

- **Background Tasks for Extracts**

This view provides information on tasks that run extracts on the Server. The view can be filtered by Extract name, Task name, Timeline, Backgrounder. There can be multiple backgrounder in Tableau Server environment.

The sheets in this View/dashboard are:

- o What extracts Ran on this Site?
- o How Much Time did Extracts Take?
- o How many extracts succeeded or failed by day?

- **Background Tasks for Non-Extract**

This view displays the tasks that are not data extract related, such as subscriptions. This view is filtered by Task name, Time Range and Backgrounder

The sheets in this View/dashboard are:

- o How Many Tasks Succeeded or Failed for this Site?
- o What Background Task Ran on this Site?

- **Stats for Load Times**

This view gives information on the time taken by View to load.

The view can be filtered by View name and Time Range.

The sheets in this View/dashboard are:

- o What are the Average Load Times for Views?
- o What are the Exact Load Times for Views?

- **Stats for Space Usage**

This view gives information on the workbooks and data sources which are consuming the most disk space.

The view can be filtered by Size of the View, Extract/Not an Extract, Object Type- Data Source or Workbook, User, Workbook name and Project name.

The sheets in this View/dashboard are:

- o What Users Use the Most Space
- o What Projects use the Most Space
- o What Workbooks and Data Sources Use the Most Space

❖ Windows **Performance monitor** can also be used for detailed performance monitoring. It is available on all windows machine. On your start program, type Performance. On Performance monitor, right click and select **Run as Administrator.**

Alerts

Email notifications can be configured for any event that occurs on the Server.

Setting up Alerts involves two steps,

- Set up SMTP Server

To send alerts, the mail server or SMTP (Simple Mail Transfer Protocol) should be configured to work with Tableau Server. SMTP setup can be done from the Tableau Configuration - **SMTP Setup tab.**

- Set up Alerts and Subscription

Alerts Configuration

Alerts and Subscription can be setup in Tableau Configuration.

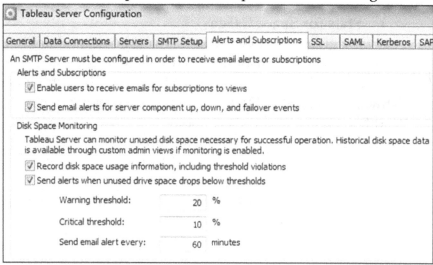

Alert and Subscription option Details

In the above screen, the Tableau Server sends an email to the recipients listed in **Send email to** on the SMTP Setup tab. Comma separated multiple email ids can be provided.

- Enable users, to receive emails for subscriptions to views. This will send emails to the user who has subscribed to the view on Tableau Server. These emails will email the updated views to the user.
- Send email alerts, for server components. This will send emails if any of the server processes Stop or Start.
- Disk Space monitoring, sends alerts about low disk space, when space on any node in a server installation drops below the configured thresholds.

8
Backup and Restore

The Tableau Administrator should perform regular maintenance tasks. These tasks would include

- Taking Regular backups
- Server Clean-up
- Prepare for Restore

Tabadmin commands are used to perform these tasks.

Tableau Server data backup

The Tabadmin backup command is used to backup Tableau Server data. If the Tableau Server data need to be restored during the upgrade or Server failure, backup created by tabadmin command can only be used.

The Backup process, backs up the content of the Tableau Server PostgreSQL database.

The Backup schedule will vary according to your organization's need, and that will depend on how often the content of the server changes.

- ❖ In case of distributed installation, backup should run on the primary machine. It will backup data from all the nodes.
- ❖ The Backup command will remove the log files older than 7 days.
- ❖ The Server can be kept running while taking a backup.

Exerccise

1. Launch command prompt as administrator and navigate to the bin directory by using

   cd "C:\Program Files\Tableau\Tableau Server\10.2\bin"

2. Use the following tabadmin command. You can provide any path or the backup file name

   tabadmin backup C:\Tableau_Backups\server -v -d

   -v option will verify the integrity of the backup
   -d will append the current data to the backup file

```
C:\Program Files\Tableau\Tableau Server\10.2\bin>tabadmin backup C:\Tableau_Backups\server -v -d
===== Using as backup tmp directory: C:/ProgramData/Tableau/Tableau Server/data/tabsvc/temp (free space: 171.66 GB)
===== Setting inheritance on C:/ProgramData/Tableau/Tableau Server/data/tabsvc/pgsql/data
===== Setting inheritance completed on C:/ProgramData/Tableau/Tableau Server/data/tabsvc/pgsql/data
===== Cleaning entries from http_requests log older than 7 days
 -- Deleted 592 rows
===== Backing up database data with tblwgadmin
===== Backing up dataengine extracts
===== Backup of database data done
===== Backup of dataengine extracts done
===== Backup written to C:/Tableau_Backups/server-2017-06-17.tsbak
===== Verifying integrity of the database backup: C:/Tableau_Backups/server-2017-06-17.tsbak
===== Unzipping pg dumps from tsbak file, this may take several minutes...
===== Setting inheritance on C:/ProgramData/Tableau/Tableau Server/data/tabsvc/temp/pg_data
===== Setting inheritance completed on C:/ProgramData/Tableau/Tableau Server/data/tabsvc/temp/pg_data
===== Restoring into test database started on port: 8061
===== Verify database completed successfully.
```

3. This command will create a **.tsbak** file in your designated directory.

❖ The Backup file also contains the configuration information about the worker nodes. If this information is not required, use the **--no -config** option. This option is useful when restore is done in a new installation environment.

❖ The Backup command removes the log files older than 7 days, if you want to keep the log files, run the following command before running the backup

   tabadmin ziplogs -l -n -f

Log files Cleanup

Before taking a backup, you may want to remove the log files and temporary files. This will ensure that the backup process runs faster and the backup file is small.

If you want to remove ALL the log files and temporary files including the current or the most recent ones, stop the server before running the clean-up command.

Restore Tableau Server

Restoring the Tableau Server is required when you are creating a new environment or when system failure occurs.

For restoring the Tableau Server data, only backups created using tabadmin backup or Tableau uninstall process are used.

When **tabadmin restore** command is used, the contents of the PostgreSQL database is overwritten with the contents of the .tsbak backup file.

If restore is done on a distributed installation, then it should be performed on the primary node.

Exercise

1. Launch command prompt as an Administrator and navigate to the bin directory by using

   ```
   cd "C:\Program Files\Tableau\Tableau Server\10.2\bin"
   ```

2. Stop the Server by using

   ```
   Tabadmin Stop
   ```

3. Use the tabadmin restore command. When this command is run, you will be asked to enter the server userid and password

   ```
   tabadmin restore C:\Tableau_Backups\ server-2017-06-17.tsbak
   ```

❖ To restore only the data but no configuration information, include the **--no-config** option

4. Restart the server

```
tabadmin start
```

❖ Backup and restore of a specific site can be done using importsite and exportsite commands explained in the previous sections.

9
Log files

While implementing the Tableau Server, you may come across several issues, and these can be resolved by gaining knowledge on different ways you can resolve a problem. Log files are helpful when you are researching an issue.

Log Files

Tableau Server generates log files for all the operations performed on the server. Log files are helpful while trouble shooting any issues.

The path to Tableau Server log directory is
C:\ProgramData\Tableau\Tableau Server\data\tabsvc\logs

Creating Archive log files

Archives of log files can be created in two ways, from the **Status** page of Tableau Server UI and by using tabadmin commands. Log file archive creates a zipped snapshot of the logs.

Creating Archive logs from the Status page

The archive created from the Status page contains logs up to seven days. In a distributed environment, it also contains the log for the worker nodes as well.

Exercise
1. Login to Tableau Server. If you have multiple sites, select **Manage All Sites** and navigate to **Status** page.

2. Navigate to **Log files** and click on **Generate Snapshot.** The Generate Snapshot option will get displayed only if no other snapshot exists.

Date generated	Size	Status
May 24, 2017, 9:08 PM	7.3 MB	Snapshot ready to download.

Generate Snapshot	Download Snapshot	Delete Snapshot

3. Use **Download Snapshot** option to download the archive.
4. Use **Delete Snapshot** to delete the existing Snapshot. You need to delete the previous Snapshot to create a new one.

Creating Archive logs using tabadmin command

Tabadmin ziplogs command copies all the log files into a zip file. On a distributed environment, this command should be run on the primary node. All worker logs will also be included in the zip file.

Exercise

1. Launch command prompt as an administrator and navigate to the location

```
cd "C:\Program Files\Tableau\Tableau Server\10.2\bin"
```

2. Stop Tableau Server

```
tabadmin stop
```

3. Create zip file by using the following command

```
Tabadmin ziplogs –l –n
```

If no file name and path are given, **logs.zip** will be created under
C:\Program Files\Tableau\Tableau Server\10.2\bin
Use –d option to only get logs after a specified date, e.g.
Tabadmin ziplogs –l –n –d 06/01/2017
-n option gets information about the ports used by the server.
-h option gives the list of all the option that can be used with tabadmin ziplogs

Tabadmin ziplogs –h

4. Restart the Server

Tabadmin Restart

Type of Log files

If you unzip the log.zip created in the previous section or if you view log files under C:\ProgramData\Tableau\Tableau Server\data\tabsvc\logs, you will see several folders.
Each of these folders contains specific log files.

Folder/file name	Description
zookeeper	Information related to the Tableau Server Coordination Service.
buildversion.txt	Contains Tableau Server's build version.
tabsvc.yml	Contains configuration changes. This file can be opened in notepad.
assetkeyencryption	Repository encryption logs.
backgrounder	Contains details about subscriptions and scheduled activities like Extract refreshes, "Run Now" tasks, and tabcmd tasks.
cacheserver	Contains details regarding the Cache

	Server Process.
clusterController	Cluster Control process logs.
dataengine	Contains information about data extracts and queries, and responses to VizQL server requests.
dataserver	Connections to Tableau Server data sources.
httpd	Apache logs. Contains authentication entries.
licensing	Contains information on different licenses.
PgSql	PostgreSQL database logs, including files related to launching server processes.
repository	Contains information on Tableau Server repository.
service	Contains details on different Services running on the Server.
solr	Contains information regarding the Search Index.
vizportal	logs related to administrative tasks, workbook and permissions, authentication, sign-ins, initial view requests, and publishing requests.
vizqlserver	Logs regarding view interaction.

Logging levels

By default, Tableau Server log files are set to **Info** level. This logging level can be changed if more details logs are required. As a best practice, log levels should not be increased, unless you are trouble shooting an issue and need additional information.

❖ Increasing the log levels can impact performance, should be used only when needed.

Tableau server log files can be set to the following levels,
- Off
- Fatal
- Error
- Warn
- Info (default)
- Debug
- Trace

Modifying the Logging levels

Logging levels can be changed by using the **tabadmin set** command. The command works with the Tableau Server component, for which you want to change the logging level. The logs are located under C:\ProgramData\Tableau\Tableau Server\data\tabsvc\logs.

In a distributed environment, the logging level must be configured on the primary machine.

Exercise
1. Launch command prompt as an administrator and type the following

```
cd "C:\Program Files\Tableau\Tableau Server\10.2\bin"
```

2. Stop Tableau Server

tabadmin stop

3. Use tabdmin set <command><option> to change the logging level for a specific component. For e.g., to change the log level for Vizqlserver, use

Tabadmin set vizqlserver.log.level trace

4. Restart Tableau Server

Tabadmin Restart

5. After gathering all the necessary logs, you can reset the logs to the default level, by using,

Tabadmin set vizqlserver.log.level -d

10
Command Line Utilities

The Tableau Server provides command line utilities to perform certain administrative and scheduling tasks.

These utilities are:

- Tabadmin
- Tabcmd

Tabadmin Utility

As we have seen in previous sections, Tabadmin commands are used to perform **administrative tasks**, such as, taking backup, zipping of log files, changing the configuration and so on. Tabadmin utility is installed automatically with the server and cannot be installed on any other machine.

How to run tabadmin commands

Tabadmin commands are always executed by launching the command prompt as an Administrator.

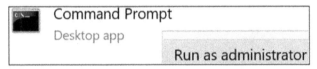

- Tabadmin commands are run from the Tableau Server installation directory. To run a tabadmin command, launch command prompt as admin and type

```
cd "C:\Program Files\Tableau\Tableau Server\10.2\bin"
```

- To get a list of all the available tabadmin commands, use

```
tabadmin help commands
```

- To get info on a specific command, type

```
tabadmin help <command>
```

- To get options for each command use, -h option. For e.g.

```
Tabadmin ziplogs -h
```

List of tabadmin commands

The following commands can be used with tabadmin utility

Tabadmin Command	Description
activate	Activates a license via online, offline or trial activation.
administrator	Grants/Revokes administrator capabilities to a user.
assetkeys	Manages asset keys that are used to encrypt keychain credentials. Provide passphrases to create keys.
autostart	Displays or sets the auto-start behavior of the Tableau Server.
backup	Creates a backup of the Tableau Server's data and configuration.
cleanup	Cleans up service log files.
clearcache	Clears cache located in cacheserver instances. Server must not be running when command is run.
Configure	Updates the configuration of Tableau Server.
customize	Sets a customization parameter to the specified value.

dbpass	Enables/disables external access to database for building administrative views.
decommission	Prepares File Store host or hosts for safe removal.
delete_webdataconnector	Deletes the specified web data connector or deletes all web data connectors from server.
desktopreporting	Cleans up desktop reporting log files.
exportsite	Exports a site's data and configuration to a file.
failoverprimary	Sets the primary and backup hosts.
failoverrepository	Failover Postgres to another worker, if available.
get	Gets the value of a configuration parameter.
get_openid_redirect_url	Gets the redirect URL from the identity provider to Tableau Server. Used when configuring the identity provider.
import_webdataconnector	Imports the specified web data connector into the server.
importsite	Imports a site from a site export file.
importsite_verified	Imports a site from an export directory with valid database mappings.
install	Installs the Tableau Server service application.
licenses	Prints information on the active licenses for Tableau Server.
list_webdataconnectors	Lists imported web data connectors by name or URL.

manage_global_crede ntials	Manages global data access credentials on Tableau Server.
passwd	Resets the password for a Tableau Server account.
prep_workers	Prepares a new worker for service. Install the software and configure it.
recommission	Revert host(s) in decommissioning state to read-write mode.
regenerate_internal_t okens	Create new versions of the security tokens that Tableau Server uses.
register	Register Tableau Server.
reindex	Rebuild search index of the Tableau Server.
reset	Reset Tableau Server state.
reset_openid_sub	Resets subs for all users or a specific user. Used when changing identity providers.
restart	Restarts Tableau Server.
restore	Restores a backup of Tableau Server's data and configuration.
sendlogs	Uploads the specified file to Tableau and associate it with a support case.
set	Sets a configuration parameter to a specified value, or to its default value.
sitestate	Sets the state of a site to a given status.
start	Start Tableau Server.
status	Prints the current running status of Tableau Server.
Stop	Stops Tableau Server.
uninstall	Uninstalls the Tableau Server service application.

upgrade	Upgrades the service configuration and data to the current version of Tableau Server.
validate	Validates environment for Tableau Server. Outputs a Rich Text Format document with the validation results.
verify_database	Verifies database integrity.
warmup	Warms up Tableau Server by requesting a lightweight viz from each vizql process.
whitelist_webdatacon nector	Adds the URL of a web data connector to server whitelist.
ziplogs	Zips up log files to the specified file. If no filename is given, "logs.zip" will be used.

Resetting Administrator password

You can reset the Administrator password using tabadmin commands

Exercise

1. Launch command prompt as an administrator and type

    cd "C:\Program Files\Tableau\Tableau Server\10.2\bin"

2. Use the tabadmin passwd <username> command

    Tabadmin passwd Administrator

    Where Administrator is the user, for whom the password is being changed.
3. The above command will prompt for a password. Enter the new password.

```
C:\Program Files\Tableau\Tableau Server\10.2\bin>tabadmin passwd Administrator
Please enter the new password for Administrator:
Please confirm the new password:
  -- Updated password for Administrator
```

Tabcmd Utility

The tabcmd commands help in automating the server tasks, such as publishing workbooks, pdf conversion, administering users, groups and so on.

When the Tableau Server is installed, Tabcmd utility gets installed in the Tableau Server bin directory
cd "C:\Program Files\Tableau\Tableau Server\10.2\bin"

You can also install tabcmd utility on any other machine. To install on any other machine, Tabcmd utility can be downloaded from https://www.tableau.com/ .

How to run tabcmd

To run tabcmd commands, follow the steps below:

1. Launch command prompt as admin and type

cd "C:\Program Files\Tableau\Tableau Server\10.2\bin"

If you are running the tabcmd from another machine, then navigate to tabcmd utility path on that machine

2. Connect to the server.

Tabcmd login -s https://localhost -u Administrator -p Admin123

❖ localhost refers to my machine and user – Administrator and password Admin123 is configured on my machine. Use settings according to your machine.

3. Run tabcmd commands

❖ If more than one task is run, each task can run one after the other in a sequence.
❖ Tabcmd command execution generates tabcmd.log. This file is located under C:\Users\<username>\AppData\Local\Tableau

List of tabcmd commands

The following commands can be used with tabcmd utility

Tabcmd Command	Description
addusers	Adds users to a group
creategroup	Creates a named group
createproject	Creates a named Project
createsitename	Creates a name site
Createsiteusers	Creates users on a site. Users are sourced from a csv file.
Createusers	Creates users on the server. Users are sourced from a csv file.
delete workbook-name or datasource-name	Deletes the named workbook or data source from the server.
deletegroup	Deletes named group from the server
teleteproject	Deletes named Project from the server

deletesite	Deletes named site from the server
deletesiteusers	Deletes users from a site. The users to be deleted are sourced from a csv file.
deleteusers	Deletes users from the server. The users to be deleted are sourced from a csv file.
editdomain	Changes the nickname or full domain name of an Active Directory domain on the server.
editsite	Changes the name of a site, webfolder, provides user management rights to Site Administrators
export	Exports a view/workbook from Tableau Server to a file. This command can also exports data used for a view.
get url	Gets the content from Tableau Server that's represented by the specified (partial) URL. The result is returned as a file.
listdomains	Displays a list of Active domains on the Tableau server.
listsites	Returns specified user's sites
login	Logs a user to the Tableau Server
logout	Logs out a user from the server
publish	Publishes named workbook, datasource or data extract to the Tableau server.
refreshextracts	Full or incremental refresh of extracts belonging to the specified workbook or data source.

removeusers	Removes users from a named group name. These users are sourced from a csv file.
runschedule	Runs the specific schedule present on the Tableau Server
set	Enables the specific setting on the server.These settings are present on the Settings page on the server.
syncgroup	Tableau Server group and Active Directory group are Synchronized. If the Tableau Server group does not exist, it is created and synchronized with the specified Active Directory group.
version	Displays the version of the current tabcmd utility

Tabcmd Global options

Global options are used by all tabcmd commands.

The --server, --user and --password options are required to begin a session.

Option(short)	Option(long)	Variable/description
-h	--help	Displays the help for the command
-s	--server	<server url>required to begin session
-u	-user	<server username> required to begin session
-p	-password	<server password> required to begin session
	--password file	<file name.txt> Allows the password to be stored in the given file.

-t	--site	<server siteid> command applies to specific site. If the site id is specified, the "Default" site is assumed. Applies to servers with multiple sites.
-x	--proxy	<host:port>uses specific http proxy
	--no -prompt	the command will not prompt for a password. If no valid password is provided the command will fail
	--no -proxy	HTTP proxy will not be used
	--no -cert- check	Does not validate the server's SSL certificate
	--[no-] cookie	the session id is saved on login. Subsequent commands will not require log in.
	--no -prefix	Will not not save the session id. By default the session is saved.
	--timeout	<seconds> Waits for specified number of seconds for the server to complete processing the command. By default, the process will timeout in 30 seconds.

Deleting a workbook using tabcmd

Follow the steps below to delete a workbook from Tableau Server using tabcmd commands

Exercise

1. Launch command prompt as Administrator and type

```
cd "C:\Program Files\Tableau\Tableau Server\10.2\bin"
```

2. Login to server, by using your server url, and userid and password

```
tabcmd login -s http://localhost/ -u Administrator -p Admin123
```

3. Delete your workbook using **tabcmd Delete**. You need to know the workbook name as on the server. If the workbook name contains a space, it will throw an error

```
tabcmd delete Superstore
```

4. Login to server and verify that your workbook is deleted.

11
JavaScript API

Tableau Javascript API is used to integrate Tableau visualizations into custom web applications. API's provide functionalities on user interaction that are not available in Tableau desktop.

The JavaScript API file is a library that contains functions for interacting with the JavaScript API.

Things you can do with JavaScript API
- On a webpage, display visualizations from Tableau Server, Tableau Public and Tableau Online
- Dynamically load and resize visualizations
- More controlled filtering
- Select Marks in visualizations
- Respond to events in visualizations
- Export visualization to an image or pdf

- To use Tableau JavaScript API, you need to have access to Tableau Server, Tableau Online, or Tableau Public, and a published workbook on that server.

Integrating Tableau Public viz in a webpage

To show an example on how to integrate Tableau public visualization in a webpage, a workbook on Tableau Public http://tabsoft.co/2u930Oa is used. From this workbook, sheet named "Line chart" will be displayed in a webpage.

See the integrated webpage on
http://www.learntableaupublic.com/tableau-javascript-api-example/

Exercise

1. Visit visualization on Tableau public by using the link http://tabsoft.co/2u930Oa.

2. Navigate to the Line chart tab and scroll down. From **share** copy the script for the **Embed Code**.

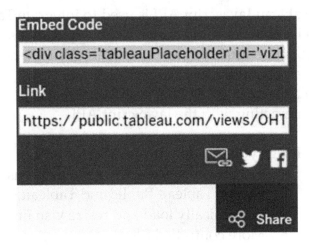

3. The above code is pasted into a blog post. To see how it appears, visit http://www.learnTableauPublic.com/javascript-api-example

Understanding the Embed code

The embed code which we took in #2 is an example of Tableau JavaScript API. Seen below, is a line-by-line explanation of the code

1. The <script> element either contains scripting elements, or it points to an external script file through src attribute. The source here points to the JavaScript API file located on Tableau Public. In this example, it is
   https://public.tableau.com/javascripts/api/viz_v1.js

   If I use visualization on my local machine, the link will be http://localhost/javascripts/api/viz_v1.js

```
<script type='text/javascript'
src='https://public.tableau.com/javascripts/api/viz_v1.js'></script>
```

2. The div tag defines a division or a section in HTML document and is used to group block elements to format them with css. In this example, we use it to define a placeholder for the object which refers to the Tableau visualization. "tableauPlaceholder" is the default css class to be used, by which the API recognizes the placeholder for the visualization. You can define the size of the placeholder using the style attribute accordingly to fit your page.

```
<div class='tableauPlaceholder' style='width: 750px;
height:600px;'>
```

3. The <object> tag defines an embedded object within an HTML document. Use this element to embed external entities like pdf, another web page, video files, etc. in your web pages. In this example, we use it to embed the Tableau view.

"tableauViz" is the default css class that the API uses to load the visualization.

The size of the object tag could be defined using width and height attributes as below.

Ensure this size does not exceed the size defined in the above div section so that the visualization fits into the placeholder accordingly.

```
<object class='tableauViz' style='display:none;'
width=750px height=600px>
```

4. You can use the <param> tag to pass parameters to plugins that have been embedded with the <object> tag.

    ```
    <param name='host_url'
    value='https%3A%2F%2Fpublic.tableau.com%2F' />
    ```

    ```
    <param name='site_root' value='' />
    ```

    ```
    <param name='name' value='OHT_Chapter11-
    Charts&#47;LineChart' />
    ```

    ```
    <param name='tabs' value='no' />
    ```

    ```
    <param name='toolbar' value='yes' />
    ```

    ```
    <param name='filter' value=':original_view=yes' />
    ```

    ```
    <param name='display_spinner' value='yes' />
    ```

    ```
    <param name='display_overlay' value='yes' />
    ```

    ```
    <param name='display_count' value='yes' />
    ```

    In this example, visualization name is OHT_Chapter11-Charts/LineChart

The complete script will look like

```
<script type='text/javascript'
src='https://public.tableau.com/javascripts/api/viz_
v1.js'></script>
<div class='tableauPlaceholder' style='width: 750px;
height:600px;'>
        <object class='tableauViz' style='display:none;'
width=750px height=600px>
                <param name='host_url'
        value='https%3A%2F%2Fpublic.tableau.com%2
        F' />
                <param name='site_root' value='' />
                <param name='name'
        value='OHT_Chapter11-Charts&#47;LineChart'
        />
                <param name='tabs' value='no' />
                <param name='toolbar' value='yes' />
                <param name='filter'
        value=':original_view=yes' />
                <param name='display_spinner'
        value='yes' />
                <param name='display_overlay'
        value='yes' />
                <param name='display_count'
        value='yes' />
        </object>
</div>
```

Object parameters for JavaScript tags

Object Parameter	Description	Examples
customViews	Hides the View button in the toolbar, which lets users save custom views.	`<param name='customViews' value='no'/>`
device	If a dashboard has layouts for mobile devices, this displays a specific layout, regardless of screen size. If this parameter isn't set, the Tableau Server or Tableau Online detects the screen size and loads a corresponding layout. See Embed Dashboards for examples.	`<param name='device' value='phone'/>`
filter	Filters the data displayed when the view opens. You can also filter using URL parameters.	`<param name='filter' value='Team=Blue'/>`
host_url	Required. The server name as it appears in the URL.	`<param name='host_url' value='http://myserver.exampleco.com/'>`
		`<param name="host_url" value="http://localhost/">`
linktarget	The target window name for external	`<param name="linktarget"`

	hyperlinks.	value="_blank"/>
load-order	When multiple views are embedded, this determines the order in which they load on the page. Negative numbers are allowed.	<param name="load-order" value="2"/>
name	Required object parameter, with this structure: [workbook name]/[sheet name]/[optional custom view name] Format optional custom view names like this: username@domain/[custom view name]	<param name='name' value='ExampleCoSales/Sales'/> <param name='name' value="ExampleCoSales/Sales/jsmith@example.com/EastRegionSales'/>
	If you refer to the Tableau Server or Tableau Online URL to confirm the value of name, exclude the session ID (:iid=<n>) at the end of the URL.	
:original_view	If the name parameter refers to a workbook or sheet URL (and does not explicitly refer to a custom view) including this parameter displays	<param name='filter' value=':original_view=yes'/>

	the view as the original view.	
path	For trusted authentication only, cannot be used with the ticket parameter. Overrides value of the name parameter and is used as the URL. For more information, see Display the View with the Ticket in the Tableau Server Administrator help.	<param name='path' value='trusted/Etdpsm_Ew6rJY-9kRrALjauU/views/workbookQ4/SalesQ4'/> http://tableauserver/trusted/Etdpsm_Ew6rJY-9kRrALjauU/views/workbookQ4/SalesQ4?:embed=yes&:tabs=yes
showShare Options	Controls whether the Share options are displayed in an embedded view.	<param name='showShareOptions' value='true' />
site_root	Required. The site name. The Default site value is null (value=''). If your server is multi-site and you want to use trusted authentication, see Display the View with the Ticket in the Tableau Server help.	<param name='site_root' value='/#/Sales'/> ance<param name='site_root' value=''/>
tabs	Displays or hides tabs.	<param name='tabs' value='yes'/>

ticket	For trusted authentication only, cannot be used with the path object parameter. Must be used with name object to construct the trusted ticket redemption URL. For more information, see Display the View with the Ticket in the Tableau Server help.	`<param name='ticket' value='9D1ObyqDQmSIO yQpKdy4Sw==:dg62gCsS E0QRArXNTOp6mlJ5'/>` http://tableauserver/trus ted/9D1ObyqDQmSIOyQ pKdy4Sw==:dg62gCsSE0 QRArXNTOp6mlJ5/view s/workbookQ4/SalesQ4?: embed=yes&:tabs=yes
toolbar	The toolbar is displayed on the bottom by default. The toolbar is placed above the view when you set this parameter to topand excluded from the embedded view when you set it to no.	`<param name='toolbar' value=top'/>`
tooltip	Tooltips are displayed by default If you set this parameter to no, however, tooltips are excluded from the embedded view.	`<param name='tooltip' value='no'/>`

12
Managing Content

Tableau server is a central repository for Projects, Groups, Users, Data sources, Workbooks, Views, Schedules and Tasks.

Data sources and Workbooks are published on the Server via Tableau desktop.
When publishing dashboards, plan on:
- Projects that will contain the Workbooks.
- Users who will have access to the dashboards.
- Users assigned to specific Groups.
- User roles and permissions.
- File types of the workbooks to be published – twb or twbx
- Data sources to be published – text files, database or TDE.

For the exercises in this chapter, use
- Tableau provided data source Sample – Superstore.xls
- Chapter12_DashboardsStory workbook. This workbook was created as part of my earlier book "Tableau 10 for Beginners". This workbook is located on Tableau Public https://public.tableau.com
- Download the workbook from http://tabsoft.co/2ppFixC. You can also create your own workbook and follow the exercises.

Create Users on Tableau Server

To perform any interaction on the Server, a user must be created on the Server/Site and assigned a role.

1. Login to Tableau Server. If it is on your local machine, then type **Localhost** on your browser, it will pop up the Tableau Server login screen.
   Login with the Administrator credentials, you have setup during installation.

```
ⓘ localhost/#/signin
```

$+\!+\!+$ **+ a b | e a u**

```
Administrator
```

```
••••••••
```

```
Sign In  →
```

❖ In Tableau, users can be added from an Active directory, can be imported from a csv file and/or can be created manually. In the trial version, you will not see the option of adding the users from an Active directory.

2. Manually create the users according to the **People** sheet in Sample – Superstore.xls. This file is located under \\Documents\My Tableau Repository\Datasources\10.2\en_US-US

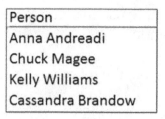

Person
Anna Andreadi
Chuck Magee
Kelly Williams
Cassandra Brandow

To create these users, click on the **Users** Tab from the top navigation bar on the Tableau Server and select **Add Users/ New User**.

- ❖ To create a Username, standard followed in this book is *First-Initial of first name and last name*
- ❖ For password, *first name (capitalized the first letter) 123 i.e. Anna123 will be the password for the first user.*
  You can create users in whatever way you want.

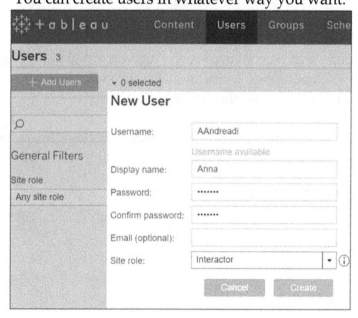

Specify the **Site role** as **Interactor**. This user can interact with the dashboard.

Different roles can be assigned to the user such as Interactor, Publisher etc.

Create the remaining users, in the same way - CMagee, KWilliams, CBrandow

❖ In this section, the following userid's and passwords are created:
AAndreadi/ Anna123
CMagee/Chuck123
KWilliams/Kelly123
CBrandow/Cassandra123

Create Groups

Groups are a way of organizing users. Business specific Groups can be created. Users are assigned to these groups. Groups can be created locally on the server or can be imported from the Active Directory.
Groups will help in implementing security. While publishing the Tableau views, you can make sure which Groups are authorized to view the specific dashboards.

1. On the Tableau server, click on the **Groups** tab and select **Add Groups**.

Groups can be created locally or imported from Active Directory. Create Local Groups Sales 1, Sales 2 and Sales 3.

❖ The **All Users** group is created by default by Tableau and all the users are added to that group.

Adding Users to the Groups

Navigate to that **Users** Tab. Check Anna Andreadi and change her Group Membership to **Sales 1**

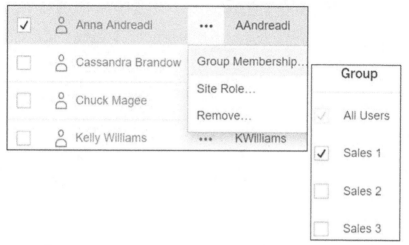

In a similar fashion, add
- Cassandra Brandow to Sales 1
- Chuck Magee to Sales 2
- Kelly Williams to Sales 3

❖ If a Group is created by importing Active Directory Group, a matching group gets created on the Server. If a member of the Active directory group does not exist on the server, it is created as a new user.
❖ If the user is removed from the Active Directory, the user is automatically removed from the Tableau Server Group and gets moved to All Users group. The user cannot login to the Server. Since the User exists on the Server, the Server Administrator has to manually delete him from the Server.

Deleting a Group

Groups, excepts for All Users group can be deleted from the server. When Group gets deleted, Users are removed from the group but are present in the Server/Site.

1. Navigate to Groups, select one or more Group/s and select Delete.

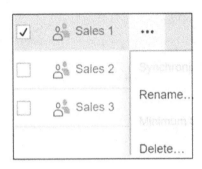

Create Projects

Projects contain related workbooks, views and data sources. Projects are related to a Site. Only the Server administrators and Site administrators, can create projects, assign permissions for projects, rename projects, and change project owners. All Workbooks must be assigned to a Project.

Two Projects - **Default** and **Tableau Samples** get created with the installation. Security can be applied to Projects as well, so that only authorized users can see a specific Project.

1. On the Tableau Server, navigate to **Content** tab from the top navigation bar.

2. Click on **New Project** and enter the name of the Project. For this exercise, say **Project: Sales1.** This Project has 0 workbooks, 0 Views and 0 Data sources.

3. In a similar fashion, create **Project: Sales2**

Move Workbook to a Project

All Workbooks must be assigned to a Project. Workbooks can be moved from One Project to another. Users having a Site role of Server/Site Administrator, Publisher or Interactor can move the Workbook. A user having Move permissions can also move a Workbook between Projects.

To move a Workbook,
1. On Tableau Server, navigate **Content** and **Workbooks**. Select a Workbook and click on **Move**. Select a Project where you want to move the Workbook.

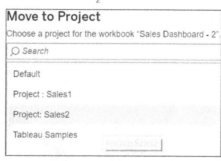

Deleting a Project

Only Server/Site Administrators can delete a Project. When a Project is deleted, all the Workbooks and Views assigned to the Project are also deleted from the Server.

1. On Tableau Server, navigate to Content and Project. Select a Project and click on Delete.

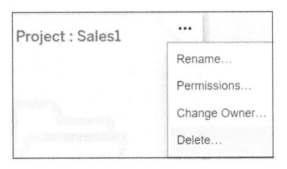

Data sources on the Server

A data source is a reusable connection information to the data sources such as excel, csv or databases etc.
Data Source connection information is created in Tableau desktop and then published to the Tableau Server.
Every Workbook must connect to a data source. While publishing a Workbook, you can specify, if the Data source will be embedded or published.

Data sources can be a connection to a data extract(TDE) or a live data. When a workbook is published as a .twbx file, the data Source is packaged with the workbook.

A **published** Data source is used to connect to multiple Workbooks. Power-Users or developers can download published data source from the server to create Workbooks.

Data Source is **embedded** in a Workbook only if the users want to connect to the data source from a single workbook.
Every published workbook will have atleast one embedded data source.

You can publish or embed a datasource while publishing a workbook from Tableau desktop

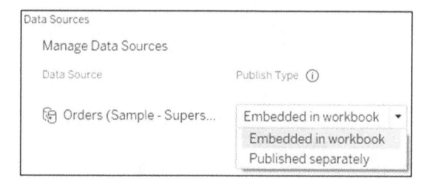

To get a list of different types of Data Sources, use the data Source filter on the Tableau Server.

Navigate to Content - DataSources and select the filters on the left.

Publishing data sources on the Server

1. Launch Tableau desktop and open Chapter12_DashboardsStory you have downloaded.
2. Navigate to any worksheet. From the left data pane, right click on the Data Source **Orders (Sample – Super Store)** and select Publish to Server

This will open up a server connect dialogue box

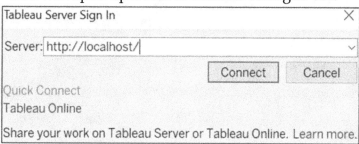

Specify your server url here. Once you click on **Connect,** you will have to provide your server userid and password.

After successful connection to the server, you will see a dialogue box **Publish Data Source to Tableau Server.**

• Provide the name of the Project.

- Provide the name of the Data source, if you want to rename the data source while publishing.
- In case of publishing an extract/TDE, specify the Data refresh schedule.
- Click **Edit** next to the permissions and specify what kind of permissions you want to give and to which Groups.
- In this example, **All Users** is given permission to connect to the data source.

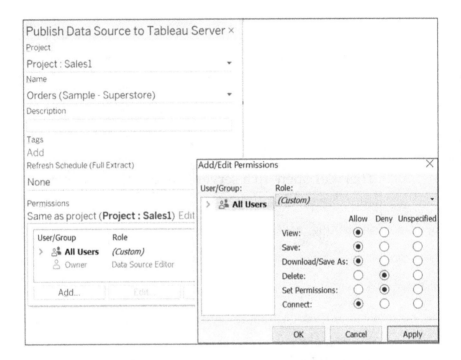

After applying all the settings, hit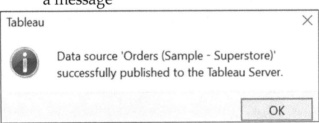
If the data source is published successfully, you will get a message

Specifying UNC path

If the data source used in the workbook is located in a network drive, a non-unc/absolute path to the data source will fail, because Tableau server will not be able to locate the datasource. In such cases you should specify a UNC path.

❖ Universal Naming Convention (UNC) specifies the location of a network resource.

Steps

1. Open your workbook in Tableau desktop. Navigate to **Data source** on the data pane.
2. Right click on the Data Source and select **Edit data source**.
3. From the **Connections** screen, select Data/edit connections.
4. Navigate to the data source in your network drive and specify UNC path as \\<network-drive location>\<datasource file name>

   E.g.

   If the workbook uses Sample-Superstore.xls located on a Network drive or path, such as **Network** Computer\folder1, use it in the following fashion

   \\Network Computer\folder1\ Sample-Supers store.xls

Working with the Data Sources

Users connecting to a data source must have **Connect** and **View** permissions on it. These permissions are required even if the user is accessing a view that connects to a data source.

To give permissions on a data source,

1. On the Tableau Server, navigate to Data Sources tab.

2. Select a Data Source,

❖ If Database drivers required for the database used in Tableau workbook, are not present on the server, they need to be installed on the Server.

Editing Data Source Connections

Server/Site Administrators or data source owners can modify the connection information of the data Source on the Server.

1. Login to Tableau Server, navigate to Content and then Data Source.

2. Select the Data Source, for which you want to update the connection information.

3. Select Edit Connection and provide Connection details
   on the **Edit Connection** screen,

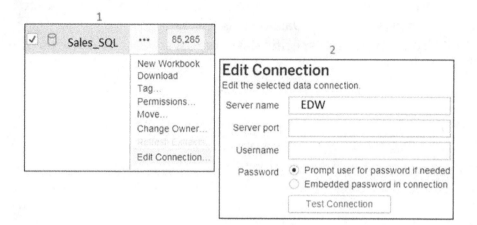

Publishing visualizations on the Server

Visualizations are created in Tableau desktop. Visualization consists of Sheets, Dashboards and Stories.
You can publish specific dashboards, sheets and stories to the Tableau Server.

* ❖ This exercise uses Chapter12_DashboardsStory workbook. This workbook was created as part of my earlier book "Tableau 10 for Beginners". You can find this workbook on Tableau Public. Download the workbook from http://tabsoft.co/2ppFixC. You can also create your own workbook and follow the exercises.

1. Launch Tableau Desktop and Open Chapter12_DashboardsStory.
From the main -menu, navigate to **Server** and select **Publish Workbook**. You may have to connect to the server, if you are not already connected.

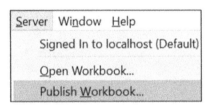

2. Views will be published to a specific **Project**, select a Project and name the published workbook.
Under sheets, you have the option to publish **Only the dashboard** or **All the sheets** or specific sheets. In this example, one dashboard and 2 sheets are published.

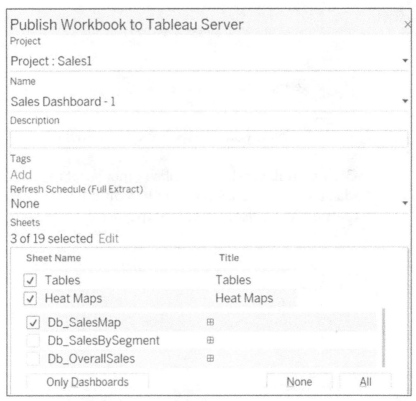

Give permission to Group **Sales 1** to view the dashboard. Leave the rest of the options as default and publish the workbook.

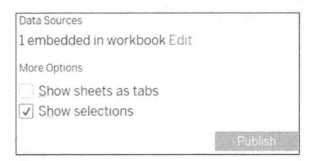

Once the workbook is published successfully, the Tableau server will be launched and a message will be displayed

Publishing Complete

▦ Sales Dashboard - 1 has been published.

On the server, you can see 3 views published.

3. In a similar fashion, publish other sheets and dashboards and assign them to a different Project. In the permissions select User/Group Sales 2

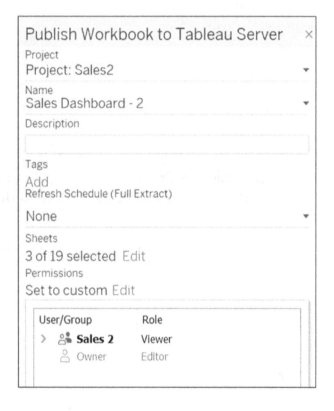

Publish Workbook to Tableau Server   ×

Project
Project: Sales2   ▾

Name
Sales Dashboard - 2   ▾

Description

Tags
Add
Refresh Schedule (Full Extract)

None   ▾

Sheets
3 of 19 selected Edit
Permissions
Set to custom Edit

User/Group	Role
> 👥 **Sales 2**	Viewer
👤 Owner	Editor

Securing Project on the Server

1. Login to Tableau Server as Administrator.

2. On **Content**, locate the **Project: Sales1** which you created in the previous exercise. You have published 3 views to this Project.

3. Hover over the Project: Sales1 box and click on the **...** in the right corner and select **Permissions**

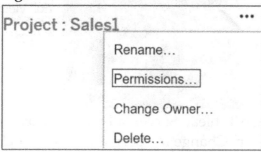

In Tableau, all Projects are by default assigned to the **All Users** group. Change "All Users" group permission to **None.**

On the same screen, from the options below, select **Add a user or group rule** and select user group **Sales 1**.

Change the permission of **Sales 1** to **Viewer**. The users in Group **Sales 1** will have viewer permission on the Project.

Securing Views on the Server

1. Login to Tableau Server as Administrator.

2. From the **Project**, go to a view. Hover over the view and click on **...** and select Permissions.

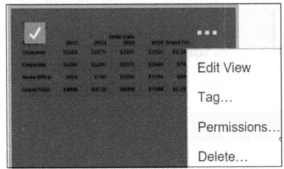

3. On Tableau Server, all views are assigned to **All Users** group. Change the permissions of **All Users**. Select **None** from the drop down.

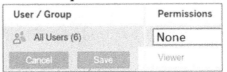

Sales 1 group will have Viewer permissions.

You can also modify the default permission of the Sales 1 Group.

Check the boxes under **View, Interact** and **Edit** depending on the type of permissions you want to provide to the Group.

This will automatically change the Permissions to **Custom**.

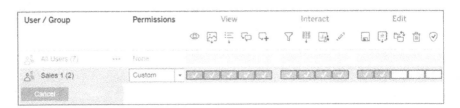

Downloading workbook from the Server

A user having Download/Save permissions on the workbook, can download a published workbook from the Server.

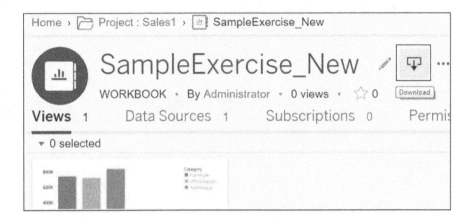

The downloaded workbook can be opened using Tableau desktop.

Performing Actions on Workbook

Depending on his permissions, a user can perform Actions on one or many Workbooks. If you have to select multiple workbooks, use the grid option on the right

Actions provide different operations on the workbook/s

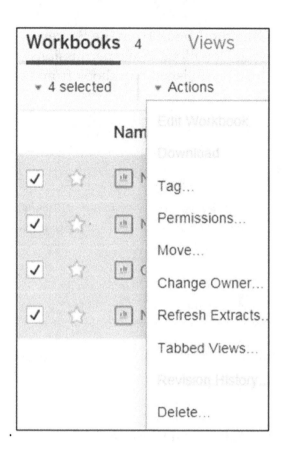

Similar **Actions** are available on other content items such as Project, View and Data Source.

Comments on Views

Users can view and post comments on a view.

Comments (1)

Sales for home office is below the threshold

Post comment

View Download Option

Based on his permissions, User may be allowed to use the download option in the view.

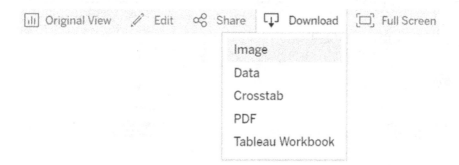

Image – Will download the view into an image file.

Data – If the user is permitted to download Views underlying Summary and Full data, he can do so using the Data option.

Crosstab – Using this option, any chart on the view can be downloaded into Crosstab.

PDF – this option will download the current view into pdf.

Tableau Workbook – This option will download the entire Workbook. This workbook can be opened in Tableau Desktop.

Data Refresh

When the underlying data of a View or Workbook changes, the user may have to manually update the View on the Server by using **Refresh** data button on the tool bar.

Sharing Views Published on the Server

Any published View can be shared or embedded into another webpage. Anyone accessing this shared view must have an account on the Tableau Server.

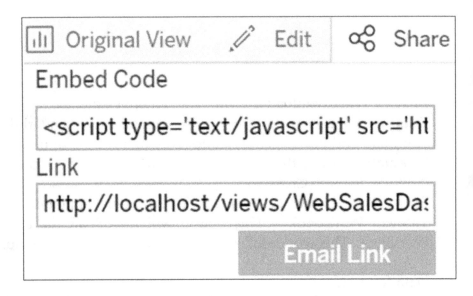

To share the view, copy and email the code in the **Link**.

To embed the view in a separate webpage, use the script in the **Embed Code**.

Scheduling and Tasks

Server and Site admins can set up schedules for data refresh and subscriptions.

Administrators can assign rights to specific users to set/create schedules. Tableau desktop publisher can set scheduled refresh tasks when they publish a data source.

❖ Developers or power users can create Data extracts using Tableau desktop. Tableau Data extracts (TDE) files are snapshot of data. You can also apply filters and create a subset of the data.

❖ Workbooks using TDE files as data source are faster as compared to the live connection to the data sources. A TDE data source can be published to the server like any other data source. Since TDE files are a snapshot of the data, they need to be refreshed once the underlying data changes. These refreshes can be scheduled on the Server.

Enable Scheduling

Scheduling must be enabled on the server, before a schedule can be set.

To enable scheduling, login as Server Admin, and navigate to **Settings**. If you have multiple sites, make sure to select **Manage All Sites** from the site drop down.

Select the check boxes under **Embedded Credentials**.

Embedded Credentials

Publishers can attach credentials to a workbook or data source. People that access the workbook or data source will be automatically authenticated to connect to data.

☑ Allow publishers to embed credentials in a workbook or data source

Publishers can schedule data extract refreshes for their workbooks and data sources to keep their extracts up to date.

☑ Allow publishers to schedule data extract refreshes

Creating a Schedule for Data refresh

1. To create a new schedule, navigate to the **Schedule** tab
2. Click on **New Schedule** and specify the **Name**, Task Type, Priority and Frequency of the schedule to run.

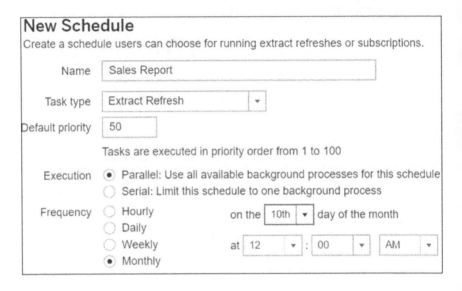

Creating a Scheduled Extract Refresh Task

A scheduled refresh task can be set for a published data source or to a workbook connected to the data extracts.

1. From **Content**, navigate to the **Data Sources** tab. Click **...** next to the data sources you want to refresh and select **Refresh Extracts**.
2. In the next **Refresh Extracts** screen, select **Schedule a Refresh** and select the schedule **Sales Report** which you created in the previous section.

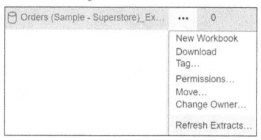

1

| Orders (Sample - Superstore)_Ex.. | ••• | 0 |

New Workbook
Download
Tag...
Permissions...
Move...
Change Owner...
Refresh Extracts...

2

Refresh Extracts

Refresh Now   **Schedule a Refresh**

Choose a refresh schedule for data source "Orders (Sample - Superstore.

Search

End of the month

Sales Report

Saturday night

Weekday early mornings

Now navigate to the Tasks and you will see your Tasks created for the Data source to refresh.

Publish a Workbook using an Extract Data source
When publishing a Workbook which uses a TDE file as a data source, you can specify the data refresh schedule. This schedule will reflect in the Server Tasks.

To publish Workbook, in Tableau desktop,
Navigate to main menu/ Server/Publish Workbook.
If you are not already connected to the Server, you need provide your connection credentials.
Provide Project name, Name of the Workbook, description and then provide the refresh data refresh schedule.
In this example, **Sales Report** schedule is selected.

Publish Workbook to Tableau Server

Project
Project : Sales1

Name
Chapter12_DashboardsStory_New

Description

Tags
Add

Refresh Schedule (Full Extract)
Sales Report (The 10th day of every month at 12:00AM)

> None
> End of the month (The last day of every month at 11:00PM)
> Sales Report (The 10th day of every month at 12:00AM)
> Saturday night (Every Sat at 11:00PM)
> Weekday early mornings (Every weekday at 04:00AM)

After publishing the workbook, login to Tableau Server and verify the tasks with this schedule.

Web Authoring

The Tableau Server administrator can grant users privileges to perform web authoring in the server environment.

- Web Authoring allows users to create workbooks from published data sources, connect to the published data sources and edit views.
- With a few exceptions, web authoring provides users almost the same functionality as Tableau desktop.
- Exceptions being, New workbooks are created only by using the published data sources. A user cannot edit the data source.

Web authoring privileges

Web authoring privileges can be provided at the **Site level** or to a specific Site user.

To provide Web authoring privilege at the site level,

1. Login as Server Admin, select a site and navigate to Settings.
2. Under Web Authoring, check Allow users to use web authoring

> **Web Authoring**
> Users with the appropriate permissions can edit workbooks in their browser.
> ☑ Allow users to use web authoring

User level privileges for web authoring

Server admin/Site admin can give a user or a group web authoring privilege.

To give this privilege to a specific user/group, give them **Web edit**, **Save** or **Download** capabilities.

1. On the Tableau Server, navigate to the Workbook and from the **...** on the right most corner, select **Permissions**

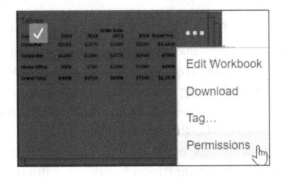

On the next **Permissions** screen, click on **...** next to the Group or user and select **Edit**

In addition to other privileges, provide privileges for **Web Edit**, **Save** and **Download Workbook/Save As**

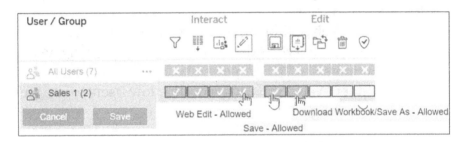

Creating views using Web Authoring

A user with web authoring privilege, can create or enhance a view.

1. In the previous exercise, we gave Web authoring access to the Group Sales. User AAndreadi (created in the earlier section) is part of the group and hence can perform Web authoring activity.
2. Login to Tableau Server as user AAndreadi or anyother user you may have created on your server for this purpose.
3. Navigate to the Data Source tab, select the data source, you want to use to create a **New Workbook**.

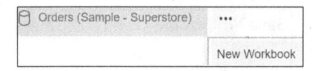

| Orders (Sample - Superstore) | ••• |
| | New Workbook |

Web authoring environment will open up in the browser. This environment will be similar to the Tableau desktop.

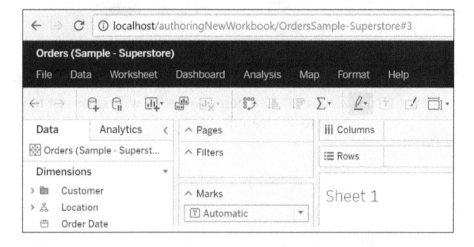

❖ The data pane has a folder and a hierarchy because it is a published data source and all these changes were done prior to publishing the data source on the server.

4. Now create couple of sheets by using Dimensions and Measures. For this example, first sheet is created by using **Category** and **Sales**. The second sheet was created with State and Sales.

5. Create a dashboard using the above sheets.

6. From the menu, select File/save as. You will be allowed to save your workbook on the server.

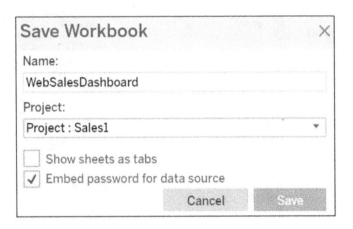

Web Authoring helps in Self-Analytics. Users can develop their own visualizations. It also helps someone who does not have access or license to Tableau desktop.

Index

About The Author

AUTHOR NAME is Chandraish Sinha
Find out more at amazon.com/author/ChandraishSinha
Or visit www.LearnTableauPublic.com

Can I Ask A Favor?
If you enjoyed this book, found it useful, or otherwise, I'd really appreciate if you would post a short review on Amazon. I do read all the reviews personally so that I can continue to improve.
Thanks for your support!